Prophets II

The Prophets of the Assyrian Period

Prophets II

The Prophets of the
Assyrian Period

Dr. G. Steve Kinnard

Prophets II: The Prophets of the Assyrian Period

ISBN: 978-0-9842006-3-4

Cover and book interior design: Toney C. Mulhollan

Illumination Publishers International
www.ipibooks.com
6010 Pinecreek Ridge Court
Spring, Texas 77379-2513

Dedication

With much love,

I dedicate this book to

Chelsea Danielle Kinnard

our first child and only daughter

"angel mine"

Contents

Contents

Acknowledgements

Thanks to...

My family, Leigh, Chelsea and Daniel. Thanks for all your love.

My publisher, Toney Mulhollan. Thanks for seeing this project through to completion.

Joan Perryman, for editing the text.

Thomas Oh, for checking the Scripture references.

Rupert and Lisa Burtan, for proofing the notes.

Cassandra Conyers, for your encouragement and help.

Randy Tinnen, Geoffrey Owens and Chris Broom, for helping with specific chapters.

John and Vivian Hanes, for computer assistance and for your friendship and encouragement.

Todd Wilson, for computer assistance.

Larry Salburg and Jerri Newman for help with editing.

Corrin Oh, for help with typing.

Art Shirley and his daughter, Ann, for scanning pages of typed material into the computer.

The elders and staff of the New York City Church of Christ, for your encouragement, friendship and support.

To the members of the Hudson Valley Region of the New York City Church of Christ, for your friendship and support over the years.

The Voice

[The village of Shofar'el in ancient Judah, c. 633 BC, the year of the coronation of Josiah, the child-king of Judah]

An entry from the personal journal of Jehoram ben Zadok

Every year I travel from my home village, just south of Jerusalem on the road to Bethlehem, to the city of Jerusalem to officiate at the temple of Solomon. I am a priest in the order of Zadok. My name is Jehoram. I enjoy this time at the temple. But I enjoy my home village far more. My village is made up of humble people who live off the land, shepherding flocks or harvesting olives and grapes.

Besides being a priest of the temple and serving as a religious functionary for my home village and the surrounding villages, I also am a keeper of bees. I harvest honey from the bees. I send my daughter to Jerusalem to sell the honey at the market. I've kept my son close to home so that I could train him in our religious writings. But now everything has changed.

Some thirty years ago, on the night of my thirteenth birthday, I received a call from the Lord. This wasn't some wandering dream of a young man. I heard the Lord's voice in my head just as plain as if my mom had called me from the field to the supper table for our evening meal. I heard the voice and it sounded like thunder on a hot summer afternoon. It was the *Kol Adonai*, the voice of the Lord, and it said, "Study the bee and harvest its honey. Raise your children in my Word because one of them will be my prophet. Listen for my voice for I will speak to you again." So, I studied the bee. I taught my son, Baruch, the Word of the Lord so he would be ready to serve. And I listened for the voice. And I listened. But the voice did not speak. I heard that voice more than thirty years ago and then silence. Silence for over thirty years. Why did he call me to prophesy and then leave me without a message?

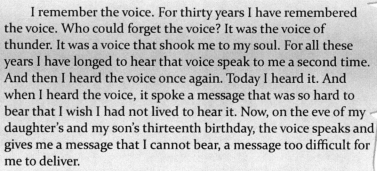

I remember the voice. For thirty years I have remembered the voice. Who could forget the voice? It was the voice of thunder. It was a voice that shook me to my soul. For all these years I have longed to hear that voice speak to me a second time. And then I heard the voice once again. Today I heard it. And when I heard the voice, it spoke a message that was so hard to bear that I wish I had not lived to hear it. Now, on the eve of my daughter's and my son's thirteenth birthday, the voice speaks and gives me a message that I cannot bear, a message too difficult for me to deliver.

So I refuse. I say to the voice, "No! I will not deliver that message. I will not be the bearer of bad tidings. I know what happens to your prophets. I know how they have to suffer. I know how much pain they have to bear. I know that their path is filled with briars and thorns and thistles. I will not declare this message. I will not deliver this word. You have made the wrong selection for your prophet. You have made a mistake."

After saying this, I shrank back. I crumbled down on the stone floor of my study. My study was pitch black. I had been praying in the darkness when I heard the voice. Now I expected a blinding light to explode. I anticipated lightning to fall from heaven and cut me down. I expected the world to open up and swallow me whole. I expected fire to consume me. I waited in expectation for the worst. I waited and I waited.

Then from the silence came the roar of thunder, and in the thunder was the voice. And the voice said, "I am the Lord your God. I am the God of Abraham, Isaac and Jacob. I am the God of Israel and Judah. I am the God of Jehoram ben Zadok. My message is my message. You are my messenger. You will deliver my message."

Then silence. No fire, no lightning, no earthquake. The voice and silence. I knew I had to obey his call. No matter how loudly I protested, I had to obey his call.

But in my heart I questioned his decision. How could this be? I had spent the past ten years preparing my son Baruch to be the prophet of God. I had toiled, teaching him the ancient

Hebrew script so that he could read the ancient scrolls. I kept him from playing with the other children so that he could memorize the Word of the Lord. I kept him out of school so that we could study the Torah. I had invested all my energy in him. I knew that he would be a great prophet for God. I knew that he would help get Judah back on her true path. I made sure that Baruch knew the story of Abraham, Isaac and Jacob. I took him back to the ancient faith of the early fathers, knowing that God would want him to be a prophet of the ancient ways.

Then God broke his silence and the voice spoke by saying, "Tell your child that I have chosen her to be my prophet." I shook my head. I silently questioned, "Chosen her?" Surely I hadn't heard correctly. So I said out loud, "Chosen her? Did you say that you have chosen her?"

The voice answered back out of the darkness, "Huldah, your first child and only daughter, will be my prophetess."

I felt a burning inside my gut. My face grew hot. I was livid. I had never been so angry. I felt deceived. I felt betrayed. I felt hurt. I shouted, "Huldah! Huldah! How could you choose my girl? I have spent all these years preparing my son to be your prophet and you choose her? She is a beekeeper. She is a market-girl. She is no leader. She has no training in the law. She can't even enter the temple. Baruch can be a prophet and priest. How could you overlook him and select Huldah?

The voice spoke back out of the darkness, "How could you overlook Huldah and select Baruch? Huldah's waters run deep. She senses things that others never feel. She is genuine. She loves me, and she loves my law. Being a prophet isn't about studying the law. It is about living the law. It is about being one with the law. Huldah knows more about the law than any student of the law, because she loves the law. Huldah will speak for me."

I protested, "But what about the suffering? What prophet have you called that hasn't suffered? What prophet have you called that hasn't been abandoned by the people? How can you ask my girl to bear that burden? Ask me, but don't ask her!"

The voice answered, "Everyone suffers. Huldah has already

suffered. She feels pain that you know nothing about. But she who suffers for what is right, suffers with hope. Through her suffering, she will offer hope to other people. Would you deny people that hope?"

"Yes!" I shouted. "If it means that she will be spared, then I would gladly withhold that hope from others. She is my girl. I'm her father. I'm supposed to protect her. I'm supposed to keep her safe."

"I too am her Father," said the voice.

"Then act like her Father," I yelled. "How could any father watch his child suffer? How could any father ask his child to walk such a torturous path?"

The voice answered, "All fathers must watch their children suffer. To grow is to suffer. To make choices means that we make painful choices. The role of the father is to teach his child how to handle the pain."

I started to cry. I knew that the voice was right. I knew he was right because I had spent the last ten years preparing my son Baruch to be ready to handle the pain. I had never considered that the voice would call my daughter. But call her he had. Now I had to tell her that she had been called to be a prophet of God.

I rose from the floor. I opened the door. I shouted toward the kitchen, "Huldah! Someone go find Huldah and send her to me!"

I rose from the stone floor. I took a couple of steps toward the fireplace. I looked in the ashes of the fireplace for an ember to light a candle. As I rose, the enormity of the moment overwhelmed me. My head grew heavy and I fell toward the floor. I remember my forehead hitting the stone floor and then blackness closed in around me.

[A few moments have passed]

From the personal journal of Huldah bat Jehoram ben Zadok

I remember the first time I heard the voice just like it was

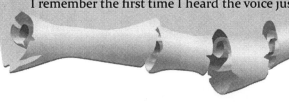

yesterday. Since that day, I have heard the voice on several occasions. But the first time the voice spoke to me was on the night of my thirteenth birthday. I'll never forget that night. But the day before my thirteenth birthday was just as eventful.

On that day I was harvesting honey from the beehives that I kept behind our home in the small village of Shofar'el. I saw someone running in the field. In my mind I asked, "Who is that running toward me? Is that my twin brother Baruch? Why would he be coming here? Shouldn't he be in the study with Abba? He had better not come any closer. He is not used to tending the bees. If he gets stung, then I'll catch all the blame."

"Baruch!" I yelled. "Stop, Baruch! Don't come any closer."

I put the cover on the bee chamber and walked over to my brother. "Baruch, why aren't you studying with Abba?"

"Huldah," Baruch said, "Abba wants to see you in his study."

"Why does he want me?" I shouted. "I've never been allowed in his study."

"How should I know?" spat Baruch, "I'm only the messenger."

"Everyone hates the messenger," I said with a vindictive tone in my voice. Then I turned and headed toward our house.

I walked into our kitchen a minute later. I saw my mother laboring over a pot of stew. Her back was to me when I entered. I didn't want to startle her, so I whispered, "Hello, Emma."

She jumped and said, "Oh, Huldah, you startled me." Then she smiled and added, "How is my almost thirteen-year-old girl?"

"Since I'll be thirteen tomorrow, you have only one more day to call me a girl," I replied. "Tomorrow I will be a woman."

"Tomorrow the world will recognize you as a woman," my mother retorted, "But you will always be my little girl. Now go see your father. He was calling for you just a moment ago."

"Why does he want to see me?" I questioned.

"I don't know," answered my mother, adding, "But he is in his study so hurry along."

I had never been in my Abba's study. He said that it wasn't a

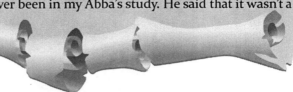

place for girls. My twin brother, Baruch, spent hours there studying the ancient scrolls that Abba had collected. Baruch wanted to
play with the other children, but Abba kept him there, laboring
over scroll after scroll. I had always wanted to study the ancient
texts, but I knew my place. My place was to keep the bees, to
harvest their honey and to sell the honey in the market. The sale
of that honey would be used to purchase more scrolls to train
my brother. Someday, he would be someone great. He would be
a leader of our people. So I endured the bee stings and the long
walks to the market to help my brother become the leader that
God wanted him to be.

As I thought these thoughts, I walked across our courtyard
to Abba's study. Every room of our house faced the courtyard.
We often kept our sheep and our donkey in this area. It was safer
for them there. I cleaned up after them. I shoveled their manure into a bucket. Then I formed patties from the manure and
placed them in the sun to dry. We used these patties for fuel for
our fires. Over these fires, we would cook our meals and boil our
water. But for now, I stepped past the animal droppings and
headed for the door of Abba's study.

The door was ajar, and it was pitch black inside. I was afraid
to enter. I knocked on the door and said, "Abba." There was no
answer. I pushed the door open just slightly and said again,
"Abba." Still there was no reply. I walked into the study. The door
closed behind me. I stretched out my arms groping in the dark. I
took short, shallow steps toward the center of the room. First my
right foot, then my left. I stopped as my foot struck something
in the floor. I reached down and realized that it was my Abba. I
stooped down and lifted his head onto my lap. My eyes had now
grown accustomed to the darkness inside the room, and I could
make out the face of my Abba. His eyes were closed and there
was a purple knot on his forehead. I lightly patted his cheek with
my hand and said in a soft voice, "Abba. Wake up, Abba. Abba,
are you alright?"

He began to stir, and he opened his eyes. I then waited for
the voice. My Abba had a voice that no one else had. It was a low,

thunderous voice that rumbled when he spoke. Everyone knew him for his voice. My friends were all afraid of his voice. If truth be told, I, his first child and only daughter, was often afraid of his voice. I had always thought that he should have been a prophet instead of a priest because he had the voice. With the voice people would have to pay attention to what he said. Now I waited for him to speak to me with the voice.

"Hello, Huldah," he said.

"Abba, are you okay?" I asked.

"Yes, dear," he replied. "I must have tripped over something and bumped my head on the floor. Help me up and I'll light a candle."

I reached under his arm and helped him stand. Using some tongs that were lying on the floor, he reached into the ashes of the fire and grabbed a glowing ember. He then took the ember to a nearby candle and lit the wick of the candle. He took the candle and used its flame to light several other candles around the room. This was my first view of his study. It was a small room with a single table along one wall. In baskets and pots around the room were dozens and dozens of scrolls and parchments. Several of the scrolls were unrolled and displayed across his table. Alongside the table were two chairs. One chair was higher than the other. It was designed for a child to be able to reach the table. In my mind I pictured Baruch sitting on the higher chair alongside of Abba as the two of them read the scrolls together.

I then looked from the chairs to my Abba's face. When I saw his face, I gasped.

"What is it, Huldah?" he asked.

"Abba, your hair! It is as white as snow." My Abba had a full head of hair and a full beard—the mark of anyone in his profession. His hair had always been black as coal except for a single patch of white hair just above his right temple. When I asked him about the white patch, he always shrugged off my question by saying; "I got that on the night of my thirteenth birthday. It was a result of listening to the voice." I had never known what he meant by that. But now his hair had gone from black to white.

It was as white as the snow on Mount Hermon. Just an hour ago it was a black as the tar pits along the Salt Sea. What was to be made of this?

He ran his fingers through his beard looking in wonderment at its change of color. "Huldah," he said, "Please sit down. I have much to discuss with you."

I sat in the smaller chair by his desk. I looked at him, anxiously waiting to hear what he had to say.

"Huldah," he began, "I'm afraid that I owe you an apology. I've been sending you to the market week after week instead of allowing you to study with Baruch."

"But Abba, " I responded, "I love keeping the bees. And as you've said, 'Honey is God's natural sweetener.' Besides, I know that we need the money, and I'm glad to be able to help provide for the family. I know that your studies with Baruch are very important. You need the money to buy scrolls and parchments."

"Huldah, please stop," said Abba frowning at me. "You mean well, but you are making this harder rather than easier. Just hear me out."

I sat in silence and focused on his voice as he continued, "Huldah, you and your brother turn thirteen tomorrow. On the night of my thirteenth birthday something extraordinary happened to me. It was an event that changed my life forever. I received a call from God. God spoke to me in words only, not in a vision or a dream. His voice sounded like thunder. I will never forget the voice."

He paused. It was a long pause. It was an uncomfortable pause. I waited patiently for him to begin again. But he stood with his back to me and his head bowed low. His face looked at the floor. I saw tears begin to fall around his feet, splashing as they struck the stone floor. I now knew why he turned his back to me. He did not want me to see him cry. Before today, I had never seen my father cry.

"Abba," I whispered. "It's all right to cry."

"Huldah," he answered, "For over thirty years I have waited to hear the voice speak once again to me. Thirty years of silence. Then today, on the eve of your thirteenth birthday, the voice spoke to me once again. And I cannot bear the message I received."

Again, I sat in silence until he continued. He wiped his eyes and turned to face me. Ink from his fingers had mixed with the tears on his face, forming black stains under his eyes. The lines at the corners of his eyes were now gullies filled with black soot from the ink. The white of his hair made the blackness of the ink even more pronounced. He stood looking down at me, and then he continued to speak.

"Huldah, you are a special girl. You come from a line of special people. You come from a line of priests in the order of Zadok. But you also come from a line of seers and prophets. God has always spoken to us in dreams and visions. On occasion, we hear the voice. My father and grandfather saw visions, but they never heard the voice. When I heard the voice some thirty years ago, my family thought that it meant that I would be a great prophet. They believed that I would speak to kings and lead our people to a great spiritual revival. I must confess that deep inside I had hoped that they were right. But over the years, that hope faded. I realized that God had not planned for me to speak to kings, but he wanted me to prepare my child for such a task. So I began training Baruch so that he would know the ancient language and the ancient texts. I felt that I had to get him ready to do God's bidding. But I was wrong. God did not choose Baruch. He chose you."

"No, Abba!" I protested. "You must have misheard. I'm a girl. I can't be a priest, so why would God call me to be a prophet. I'm just a beekeeper and a market-girl. I'm no leader. Why do you think that God has chosen me?"

"Because Huldah," he answered, "I made the same protests to God that you just made to me. And the voice said to me, 'Huldah's waters run deep. She senses things that others never

feel. She is genuine. Huldah, your first child and only daughter, will be my prophetess.'"

"The voice said that?" I asked.

"Yes, he did," Abba answered.

"And he said, 'first child, only daughter?'"

"Yes."

My stomach began to turn sour. Sweat started to bead up on the palms of my hands. My head grew faint. I could feel my heart beating faster. I wanted to run. I wanted to run and keep running until I was far, far away. But my legs were frozen. My feet felt like lead. This phrase, "first child, only daughter" was my phrase. It was the phrase that I had used for as long as I could remember to identify myself. It was my badge of honor. For the voice to use that phrase meant that there could be no mistake. For my Abba to use that phrase meant that he wanted me to understand the seriousness of this conversation.

With a quivering voice I said, "Abba, I'm scared."

Abba came and sat down beside me. He put his arm around me and pulled my head over onto his shoulder. With a soft voice he began to sing me songs that he once sang when he put me to sleep at night. These songs had a way of making me feel safe. Time passed. Finally Abba spoke, "Huldah, I think I've run out of songs."

"Abba," I said. "What does all this mean?"

"I wish I knew," he said. Then he added, "More than thirty years ago the voice said to me, 'Study the bee and harvest its honey. Raise your children in my Word because one of them will be my prophet. Listen for my voice for I will speak to you again.' Then silence for more than thirty years. The Lord is God. He makes his plan in his own time and in his own way. I'm not sure what this means for you. But two things I do know.

"One is that with the task of being a prophet comes ridicule and suffering. When I was a boy and people perceived that God had spoken to me, my friends withdrew from me, my teachers spoke down to me and my family expected me to be perfect. That's

why I kept Baruch separate from the other children and out of school. At some point you will have to suffer. Because that's what prophets do best, they suffer. Have you ever heard the phrase, 'Everyone hates the messenger?'"

I chuckled, "Yes, I've heard it once or twice."

"Well, it's true." He said. Then he added, "A second thing I know. You will be ready for the task. I'll help you get ready. But even if I were not around, I know that you would get yourself ready. You've always been a deeply spiritual girl. I remember some of the older girls who sat with you when you were young shared with me, "Huldah was sharing her dreams with us and her dreams were filled with heavenly beings and images from beyond this world.' I didn't think much of this at the time. I thought they were the product of a healthy imagination. I've always thought of you as an artist. Now I know that you have the ability to see beyond this world. You are connected to the heavenly realm in a special way.

"Then there was your eighth birthday. We had a party for you and your brother in the courtyard. You were just beginning to open your presents when a few drops of rain began to fall from the sky. Without any hesitation and without anyone's prompting, you dropped your head and said a prayer, 'Dear Adonai, if it must rain today, please don't let it rain until the evening because my party will be over by then.' The raindrops stopped. As evening approached, after all your guests had gone, the heavens opened with the most powerful rainfall I've ever seen.

"You have always been a deeply spiritual girl. Now your gift, your spirituality, will be God's gift to our nation.

"Huldah, God has chosen you to do great things for him. But that call comes at a price. You will never be just one of the girls. I know that you've wanted that. I know there are times that you've hated being the daughter of a priest. You've hated feeling like you have to live your life to meet the expectation of the families around us. But now you must see that you're no longer 'the

priest's daughter.' You are 'God's daughter.'

"Stay true to who you are inside. Don't worry about what other people think of you. You will always feel things more deeply than most people. You will always think differently than most people. That is your special gift. See it as a gift and not as a curse. Be encouraged and not burdened by it."

"Huldah, I want to give you something that my Abba gave to me on my thirteenth birthday. To be honest with you, I had meant to give it to Baruch, but you should have it."

He walked over to one of his shelves, stretched his arms up to the top shelf and pulled something off of it. He brought it over and sat it in my lap. It was a model of the temple of Solomon that had been meticulously carved from solid alabaster.

"Huldah," Abba said. "This was made by one of our ancestors during Solomon's reign. He too was a priest of the temple. Open it up."

I took the lid off the top of the temple and the inside of the temple was carved just as meticulously as the outside. I peered into the Holy of Holies and saw a miniature carving of the Ark of the Covenant.

"Huldah," said my Abba, "The temple is in great need of restoration. I don't think it will happen in my lifetime. But this year a new king has been crowned. An eight-year-old child-king named Josiah. Perhaps he will restore the temple to its former glory. If he starts to restore the temple, then be sure that you give him this model so that he will know how glorious the temple looked during Solomon's reign.

"But also let him know that the temple isn't the only thing that needs to be restored. Our worship needs to be restored. We have lost touch with the ancient ways. I keep reading in the ancient texts about a Book of the Law. It comes from the time of Moses and is filled with the ancient ways of worship. That is why we must study the ancient texts. If the Book of the Law is ever found, then it will be written in the ancient script and the

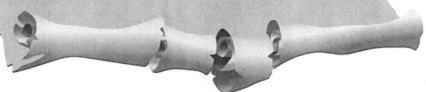

ancient dialect that has long gone out of use. You must be able to
read the ancient script so that you can identify the Book of
the Law. You must understand the ancient dialect of Abraham
and Moses. Are you ready for your first lesson?"

"Yes, Abba," I replied.

"Just sit and listen while I read an ancient scroll written
in the ancient script and the ancient dialect. Listen to how our
language sounded during the time of Moses."

He began to read. As he read, I listened. I listened, but I
couldn't understand the words. The words weren't important to
me. The important thing was that he was reading the ancient
text to me. To me, his first child and only daughter. I listened,
not to the words, but to his voice. His voice. A voice that children
in my village called, the voice.

The next day was my thirteenth birthday. On the night of
my thirteenth birthday, a voice like the sound of thunder woke
me from my sleep. It was the voice. The voice called me to be his
prophetess.

When I awoke the next morning, I saw my Abba in the
kitchen. "Hello, Abba," I said. As he turned to look at me, Abba
said, "Happy Birthday!" Then, he paused. As he looked at me,
his expression changed. He had a look of surprise, which
turned into a look of understanding.

"Huldah, have you looked at yourself this morning?" he
asked.

I ran over to a large jar of water that sat on the kitchen floor.
As I peered at my reflection in the water, I saw that a patch of
hair just above my right temple had turned white—white as
the snow on Mt. Hermon. I looked at my Abba and smiled. He
smiled back at me. We both knew that I had heard the voice.

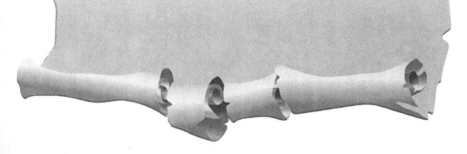

Introduction

I began this work in the late eighties. I studied the prophets because I wanted to be more like the prophets. I love the prophets of Israel. The prophets have changed my life. Each time I pick up one of the prophetic books, I get excited. They speak to my soul. They make me a better person.[1]

My study of the prophets resulted in a three-volume manuscript on the prophets of Israel, which I finished in November of 1993. I published the first volume of this manuscript with Discipleship Publications International in 2001. In the introduction to that book, I wrote, "This book has been a labor of love. It represents more than thirteen years of my life—five years of study and research to write it and another eight to publish it. During those years I have been drawn closer to God through the vision of the prophets."

You can add nine more years to the above because it's almost 2010, and I'm now getting the second volume out. If you haven't read the first volume, it serves as an overview to the prophetic literature of the Bible. You don't have to read the first volume before you read this one, but it might be helpful to do so.

This volume begins with two prophets of uncertain date:

Joel: The Prophet of Zion's Future
Obadiah: The Prophet of Sovereignty

The book then discusses the prophets of the Assyrian period beginning with Amos and ending with Micah. The prophets of the Assyrian period prophesied concerning the decline and fall of the Northern Kingdom of Israel. This was an extremely turbulent time for the people of Israel and Judah. We will look at the five prophets of this period in this order:

Amos: The Prophet of Social Justice
Jonah Ben Amittai: The Prophet of God's Universal Love
Hosea Ben Beeri: The Prophet of Unconditional Love
Isaiah Ben Amoz: The Prophet of Holiness
Micah of Moresheth: The Prophet of the Poor

This book contains a critical introduction to each of the above-mentioned prophets. These introductions do not serve as a substitute for reading the Biblical text, but as a help to understanding the text. The student should read this introduction alongside the Bible.

Each section contains material that clarifies what is occurring in the Biblical text. The material begins with an overview, moves to more detailed information, and closes with a practical lesson. It is hoped that other ministers and teachers can use this material to teach the prophetic books in their churches. Historical, political, archaeological and geographical material is found alongside theological teaching. The chapters are divided as follows:

1. Date
2. Location
3. Purpose
4. Theme
5. Meaning of Name
6. Audience

Throughout the book, I refer to the God of Israel by the name "Yahweh." I believe this name comes much closer to the pronunciation of the name revealed to Moses on Sinai than Jehovah does. I prefer it to Jehovah; therefore, it will be found throughout this book.

I have used a number of different translations in this work. My primary translation was *The Revised Standard Version*. Unless noted in the text, this is the translation being used. Other translations were used and their abbreviations are listed as follows:

NEB—*The New English Bible*
NIV—*The New International Version*
JB—*The Jerusalem Bible*
Tanakh—*Tanakh–The Holy Scriptures: The New Jewish Publication Society Translation According to the Traditional Hebrew Text*
PB—*The Poet's Bible*

I pray that this book helps you to appreciate and understand the written prophets of the Assyrian period. I know that this type of study can be a life-changing study. I know that because the prophets changed my life.

—GSK, December 2009

The Written Prophets

Prophets of Uncertain Date

Joel	Prophet to Judah
Obadiah	Prophet to Israel/Judah concerning Edom

The Decline and Fall of Samaria
8th century BC — The Assyrian Period

Jonah	c. 780–740	Prophet to Nineveh
Amos	c. 786–742	Prophet to the North
Hosea	c. 750–715	Prophet to the North
Isaiah	c. 742–696	Prophet to the South
Micah	c. 740–710	Prophet to the South

The Decline and Fall of Judah
7th century BC — The Babylonian Period

Pre-Exilic Prophets

Zephaniah	c. 621	Prophet to Judah
Nahum	c. 615–612	Prophet to Judah
Habakkuk	c. 612–605	Prophet to Judah
Jeremiah	c. 626–562	Prophet to Judah

The Exile
6th century BC — The Babylonian Period

Daniel	c. 605–536	Prophet to Jews in Exile
Ezekiel	c. 592–571	Prophet to Jews in Exile

The Restoration
6th century BC — The Persian Period

Haggai	c. 520	Prophet to the Jews after the Exile
Zechariah	c. 519–518	Prophet to the Jews after the Exile
Malachi	c. 445–435	Prophet to the Jews after the Exile

SECTION ONE

Two Prophets
of Uncertain Date

Joel Ben Pethuel
The Prophet of Zion's Future

Obadiah
The Prophet of God's Sovereignty

Some scholars date Joel as a pre-exilic book. They believe that Joel is describing a situation in Jerusalem that existed before the exile. Jerusalem is viewed as being in a fairly stable situation (yet impending doom awaits the city). Douglas Stuart, author of *Hosea-Jonah* in the Word Biblical Commentary, writes:

> Ultimately, however, any dating of the book of Joel can be only inferential and speculative. It is on the basis of the sorts of conditions apparently reflected in the prophecy that one assigns a tentative date. ...Our assumption is that Joel is a unified work composed under the circumstances of an invasion against the city of Jerusalem (and thus, of course, Judah) by Mesopotamian enemy forces, either Assyria or Babylonia. If this admittedly speculative assessment is correct, the words of the book would likely have been spoken on one of these occasions: the Assyrian invasion of 701 BC, the Babylonian invasion of 598 BC, or the Babylonian invasion of 588 BC.[3]

Not many scholars hold to a pre-exilic dating of Joel.

Most scholars believe the book of Joel was written after the exile. The book seems to be describing Jerusalem after the exile in Babylon. The temple (1:14) and the walls of the city (2:9) have been rebuilt. The worship of the cultus has been restored and the priests are once again the most prominent officials in the city (1:13). These conditions point to a post-exilic date sometime around the year 400 BC for the prophetic activity of Joel.

If we could precisely date the locust plague described by Joel, then we could give the book an exact date. But since we cannot precisely date the locust plague, we cannot give an exact date for the book. Therefore, we place it and Obadiah in the category of prophets of an uncertain date.

2. Location: Jerusalem in Judah

3. Purpose

With the use of a terrible locust plague that devastated the countryside, God depicted the Day of Yahweh as a day of destruction during which he would avenge himself against his adversaries (1:15; 2:1; 3:1, 19-32; 4:14).

4. Theme: The Day of the Lord is a day of destruction and a day of hope.

5. Meaning of Name

The book is attributed to *Yoel* son of Pethuel. His name is also that of twelve other men in the Old Testament and means "Yahweh is God."

6. Audience: Judah and Jerusalem

7. Outline

> I. The Scourge of Locusts and Drought and the Call to Repentance, 1:1-2:17.
>
> A. Extent of the plague, 1:1-12.
> B. Call to repentance, 1:13-20.
> C. Extent of the plague; the approaching day of divine wrath, 2:1-11.
> D. Call to repentance, 2:12-17.
>
> II. Promise of Blessings Through Restoration, 2:18-3:21.
>
> A. Deliverance from the locusts, material blessings, 2:18-3:21.
> B. The outpouring of the Spirit, spiritual blessings, 2:28-32.
> C. Judgment upon the nations; blessings for the glorious future of God's people, 3:1-21.

8. Memory Work

Joel 2:12-13

"Yet even now," says the Lord,
    "Return to me with all your heart,
with fasting, with weeping, and with
    mourning;
and rend your hearts and not
    your garments."
Return to the Lord, your God,
    for he is gracious and merciful,
slow to anger, and abounding in
    steadfast love,
    and repent of evil.

Joel 2:28-29

And it shall come to pass
    afterward,
that I will pour out my spirit on all
    flesh;
your sons and your daughters shall
    prophesy,
your old men shall dream dreams,
  and your young men shall see visions.
Even upon the menservants and
    maidservants
in those days, I will pour out my
    spirit.

Joel 3:9-10

Proclaim this among the nations:
Prepare for war,
    stir up the mighty men.
Let all the men of war draw near,
    let them come up.
Beat your plowshares into swords,
    and your pruning hooks into
    spears;
let the weak say, "I am a warrior."

Joel 3:13
Put in the sickle,
    for the harvest is ripe.
Go in, tread,
    for the winepress is full.
The vats overflow,
    for their wickedness is great.

Joel 3:14
Multitudes, multitudes,
    in the valley of decision
for the day of the Lord is near
    in the valley of decision.

9. Special Note

Since the locust plague Joel describes in 1:2-2:17 cannot be dated with any historical accuracy, many scholars deny the occurrence of such a plague and refer to it as a literary allusion. Joel himself presents the plague as being historical. In fact, it is the basis for the writing of his prophecy. There seems to be no solid reason for denying the historicity of the attack of locusts. This type of phenomenon was quite common in Palestine during the days of the Old Testament. In fact, it is still quite common today.

A locust attack was a horrendous event. Craigie, in his commentary on the Minor Prophets, quotes from the *National Geographic* magazine of December 1915 describing a locust attack:

> At the end of February, great clouds of locusts began flying into the land from a northeasterly direction, so that attention was drawn to them by the sudden darkening of the bright sunshine. They came in enormous numbers, settling on the fields and hillsides. There they laid their eggs in vast numbers (it was calculated that some 60,000 could come from the eggs planted in thirty-nine square inches of soil, and that figure involved a 30% loss rate!) Once hatched, the new broods started crawling across the ground, at a rate of 400 to 600 per day, devouring every scrap of vegetation in their path.[4]

This type of devastating attack was common in the Middle East. In fact, the locust attack of 1865 AD in Jerusalem was so devastating that 1865 is still known as "the year of the locusts."

10. Historical Context

Joel prophesied during a time of political and economic calm for Judah. The people were not concerned with outside threats to their security. The sudden locust attack upon the land as described in the first two chapters of Joel came as a surprise. Joel used this situation to awaken the people from their stupor. He compared the attack of the locusts to the sudden coming of the day of the Lord—a day of destruction for God's enemies and a day of hope for God's faithful people.

11. The Person

The Bible states that "the Word of Yahweh came to Joel" (1:1), thus attributing the book to him. However, very little is known about the author except what can be gained from the book itself. We do know that Joel was "the son of Pethuel" although it is impossible to identify Pethuel.

Since Jerusalem is the focal point of the book, Joel was probably a resident of that city. It is possible that he was a priest or a cult-prophet of the temple of Jerusalem. We do know that he received "the Word of the Lord" and served as a prophet for a short period of his life. We can assume from the beautiful poetry and literary power of the book that Joel was a man of some education. He was familiar with the work of the prophets before him and alludes to their work in his book. Other than these scant facts, we have no other information about the life of Joel.

12. The Call

Nothing is known of the call of Joel except what is given in the opening statement of the book, "The Word of the Lord that came to Joel, the son of Pethuel." How old was Joel when he was called? What was his profession when he was called? How did he react when he was called? All these questions remain a mystery.

13. Structure and Form

Joel composed four prophetic oracles that are of moderate length compared to the oracles of other Old Testament prophets. These oracles are well constructed, being short enough to cover just one or two themes and long enough to allow for some repetition as a memory device. Stuart notes:

> Joel is also somewhat more tightly organized than many of the prophetic books, with such a degree of thematic and vocabulary linkage among the pericopes, and a logical progression from one pericope to the next, that it is reasonable to conclude that Joel's message was originally composed and delivered either at one time or in a relatively short span of time (perhaps a week or a month).[5]

However long it took him to write the book, Joel leaves us one of the most beautifully and carefully constructed books of the Hebrew canon.

14. Theology
A. The Day of the Lord is a Day of Judgment.

Joel uses a theme that is also used by Amos (the day of the Lord) and applies it to his situation. The Day of the Lord will not be a day of national restoration or a day of realized hope for Israel—instead it will be a day of punishment. Israel had rebelled against God. God's justice requires punishment for Israel's rebellion. The Day of the Lord would be the realization of this retribution. Joel 2:1-2 describes this day:

> *Blow the trumpet in Zion;*
> *sound the alarm on my holy*
> *mountain!*
> *Let all the inhabitants of the land*
> *tremble,*
> *for the day of the Lord is coming,*
> *it is near,*

> *a day of darkness and gloom,*
> *a day of clouds and thick*
> *darkness!*

The term "day of the Lord" (*Yom Yahweh*) occurs five times in Joel (1:15; 2:1, 11, 31; 3:14) and is found in each of his four oracles. This theme is the driving force of the book. In the first half it is used as a rallying cry to call Judah to repentance. In the second half of the book it is used as a national anthem to remind the people of God's deliverance from the foreign powers. Whereas once the day of the Lord was a day of national disaster for unrepentant Israel, it would become a day of national celebration for the people of God.

The day of Yahweh has its origin in the concept of the Israelite Holy War. The Jews believed that the Sovereign Lord could demand respect from his people (or any people) by conquering them in a single day. In the first half of Joel, God demanded respect by sending an army into his land to discipline his people. In the second half, the army of God marched against the foreign powers, bringing them into submission. The first event did not necessarily have to occur. Israel could have averted disaster through repentance. Once the first event happened, the second event had to occur at some point in the future. The only question left to answer was when the day of the Lord would come.

B. Repentance Can Avert Disaster

As has been noted above, the national disaster that awaited God's people in the *Yom Yahweh* (day of the Lord) could be averted through repentance. The repentance must not be an outward ceremonial repentance, but it must be true repentance of the heart. Joel 2:12-14 states:

> *"Yet even now," says the Lord,*
> *"return to me with all your heart*
> *with fasting, with weeping, and with*
> *mourning;*

and rend your hearts and not
    your garments."
Return to the Lord, your God,
    for he is gracious and merciful,
slow to anger, and abounding in
    steadfast love,
        and he repents of evil.
Who knows whether he will not turn
    and repent, and leave a blessing behind him,
a cereal offering and a drink offering
    for the Lord, your God?

Repent or disaster will come. Repentance is urgent. So urgent that the nation is called to fast. When a solemn assembly is called, even the nursing mothers and newlyweds are expected to attend (Joel 2:15-16). If the nation will urgently repent, then not only will the disaster be averted, but God will take back his curse and bless the land. Repentance averts disaster and produces blessing.

This type of solemn assembly and corporate repentance can still be used today among God's people. At times, we can grow complacent, our zeal can wane and our enthusiasm can grow cold. Selfishness can overtake our lives. We can lose focus on what is really important in life. During these times there is a need for revival. Joel gives us a grand model for revival in chapter 2. We must assemble the church and rend our hearts with fasting and weeping and mourning. God hears our cries of repentance and blesses us when we repent.

15. Messianic Expectations

The book of Joel is highly apocalyptic in nature. It looks to the future through symbolic language that describes a time when God will usher in a new age. The New Testament writers pick up on Joel's apocalyptic language and use his writing to substantiate the fact that they were living in the new age. The most obvious use of Joel in this manner is found in the writing of Luke in Acts

2 where Luke views what transpired on Pentecost as a fulfillment of Joel 2:28-32. Peter quotes this section of Joel in its entirety in his speech in Acts 2. The outpouring of the Spirit in Acts 2 is seen as a direct fulfillment of the outpouring of the Spirit in Joel 2. This means that the New Testament writers saw Acts 2 as the inauguration of the first-century day of the Lord. A new age of God's rule began on the first Pentecost after the resurrection of Jesus.

16. Important Passages
Joel 3:9-21—People Get Ready

People get ready, there's a train a-comin'
You don't need no baggage, you just get on board
All you need is faith to hear the diesels hummin'
Don't need no ticket, you just thank the Lord
                    —Curtis Mayfield, singer/songwriter

Joel 2:28-32 describes the upcoming day of the Lord as a day in which God would usher his kingdom into the world. This day would come unexpectedly. Everyone must be ready for the day of the Lord to come. If not, then this day of joy and celebration would be a day of disaster and gloom. How does Joel prepare God's people for that day? What must we do to be ready for Day of the Lord?

I. Prepare: 3:9-12
    To be ready for the day of the Lord one must prepare for it. This is not a once in a lifetime preparation. It is a daily preparation. Spirituality is a daily endeavor.

What does it take to be prepared?

    (1) Time. One must invest time to be prepared. If you desire to learn the classical guitar, you will have to devote time to

master it. To really master it, takes daily practice. I once knew a wonderful classical guitarist. His hands would glide across the strings causing a cascade of music to flow from his instrument. How did he achieve this expertise? It took time. He told me that he has been practicing at least four hours a day for years. He would go over the same musical phrase dozens of times until he got it exactly like he wanted it. There were no shortcuts.

Anything worthwhile in life requires a time commitment. To be ready for the day of the Lord we have to give time to our relationship with God. Bible study and prayer will not be excellent unless consistent time is devoted to them. Our relationships with others take time as well. We will never be close to anyone unless we give him or her our time. There is nothing more satisfying than seeing someone become a disciple. This satisfaction comes out of investing yourself to help them change. This takes time, but it is time well spent. Getting ready for the *Yom Yahweh* takes time. And if we aren't ready for it, then we have wasted all of our time.

Of course time is only one ingredient of our investment to be ready for the Day of the Lord. We also have to obey God by righteously following his laws. We have to walk closely with him every single day. God is looking for hearts that are desirous of him. He will reward those who earnestly follow him.

(2) Effort. To prepare for the kingdom takes time, and it also takes effort. God's grace does not stand in opposition to effort on your part. You don't earn salvation, but you must put effort into living a righteous life. You never get something for nothing. This is as true in your spiritual life as it is in other areas of life. When I asked my wife to marry me, I knew it had to be a special occasion. We both lived in Raleigh, North Carolina at the time. I had very little money, but I knew I had to make things great. We went out to the best steak restaurant in Raleigh and we splurged on a great dinner. Then I took her to our favorite park in Raleigh. Along a pond in the park was a gazebo that looked out across the water. We sat together watching the moonlight dance across the pond. I had prepared a song for her earlier in the week, in which

I proposed marriage. I had written the song on special paper and framed it. At the right moment I gave her the framed lyrics and began to sing the song. On the last line of the song I got down on one knee, reached in my pocket and pulled out an engagement ring, and sang; "Now I ask on bended knee, Leigh, will you marry me!" She was so taken back that it took her a couple of minutes to respond. The look of shock on her face was worth all the effort that had gone into making the evening great.

We understand the need for effort in many areas of our lives. Why is it that when it comes to our relationship with God, we want to take the easy road? The road to the kingdom is straight and narrow. It is difficult. We have to make sacrifices for God. Without the effort, we will not make it.

II. Respond: 3:13
> *Put in the sickle,*
> *for the harvest is ripe.*
> *Go in, tread,*
> *for the winepress is full.*
> *The vats overflow,*
> *for their wickedness is great.*

Joel teaches us a valuable lesson—when the harvest is ready, the crops must be harvested. You must respond. There is no time to waste at harvest time. Wasted time means a loss of crops. The crops will literally rot on the vine. I grew up in Middle Tennessee. Every summer I planted a garden. It was usually a small garden with a few radishes, several okra plants and plenty of tomatoes. When tomatoes are ready to be picked, you can't delay. Once we went away on vacation just as the tomatoes were ripening. When we arrived back home, dozens of tomatoes had rotted on the vine. For a real "tomato lover," it was a depressing homecoming.

When the harvest is ready, you must swing the sickle. You must respond. God decides when the harvest is ready. He says, "Swing the sickle," and we respond. He will declare when the harvest is ready. Our task is to respond to his declaration. A prophet responds to God's call. Are you ready to respond to God's call?

III. Appreciate the Results: 3:14-21

To be ready for the day of the Lord, you have to be thankful for everything God has done for you in your life. God promises that he will bless us. Are we grateful for God's blessings? Do we take inventory of everything that God has done for us? We should. We need to be like children who enjoy the least little gift. Let's always remember to thank him for what he has done for us.

᭦ ᭦ ᭦

Being ready for the Day of the Lord is a daily decision. Sometimes we get so out of touch with the reality of our spiritual lives that we grow complacent. Just like a car engine that has not been started in months, we need to be jump-started. I remember in the beginning of 1993, I needed such a jump-start. I had grown complacent. I felt I was out of tune spiritually. It's not that I was committing some major sin. I just felt really sluggish in my relationship with God. My Bible study was stale. My evangelism was an effort. The ministry was a burden. Things needed to change.

I decided to start the year with a forty-day fast on fruit and vegetable juices—nothing but juice and water. I knew that to make it forty days without eating I was going to have to depend on God. I prepared my mind. I bought a juicer and got ready for the fast. I read verses on fasting and set my mind. I pursued my goal. It was not easy, but I never gave up. I often wanted to eat. At the movies I always wanted to cheat by grabbing some popcorn. But I kept fasting, and I never cheated. At the end of the first month, I felt so great that I extended the fast an extra month. I went sixty days instead of forty. At the end of the fast I felt greater than I had ever felt in my life. God blessed me, and he blessed my ministry. I thanked God for seeing me through to the completion of my goal. The jump-start that I needed had occurred. It occurred because I prepared my mind, pursued my goal and appreciated the victory that God gave me.

Sequentia
Wolfgang Amadeus Mozart

Day of wrath, that day
Will dissolve the earth in ashes
As David and the Sibyl bear witness.

What dread there will be
When the Judge shall come
To judge all things strictly.

A trumpet, spreading a wondrous sound
Through the graves of all lands,
Will drive mankind before the throne.

Death and Nature shall be astonished
When all creation rises again
To answer to the Judge.

A book, written in, will be brought forth
In which is contained everything that is,
Out of which the world shall be judged.

When therefore the Judge takes His seat
Whatever is hidden will reveal itself.
Nothing will remain unavenged.

What then shall I say, wretch that I am,
What advocate entreat to speak for me,
When even the righteous may hardly be secure?

King of awful majesty,
Who freely savest the redeemed,
Save me, O fount of goodness.

Remember, blessed Jesus,
That I am the cause of Thy pilgrimage,
Do not forsake me on that day.

References

Allen, L. *The Books of Joel, Obadiah, Jonah and Micah*. New International Commentary on the Old Testament. 1976.

Baker, D., D. Alexander and B. Waltke. *Obadiah, Jonah, Micah*. Tyndale Old Testament Commentary, 1988.

Bewer, J. A. A *Critical and Exegetical Commentary on Obadiah and Joel*. International Critical Commentary. 1911.

Cole, R. "Joel." In *The New Bible Commentary Revised*. Edited by D. Guthrie and J. Moyter. 1970. 716-725.

Driver, S. R. *The Books of Joel and Amos*. The Cambridge Bible for Schools and Colleges. 1897; Second Edition, 1915.

Gangi, M. D. *The Book of Joel*. Shield Bible Study Series. 1970.

Koch, K. *The Prophets, Vol. 1, The Assyrian Age*. 1982.

Mason, R. *Micah, Nahum, Obadiah*. 1991.

Wade, G. *The Books of the Prophets Micah, Obadiah, Joel and Jonah*. Westminster Commentaries. 1925.

Watts, J. D. W. *The Books of Joel, Obadiah. Jonah, Nahum, Habakkuk and Zephaniah*. The Cambridge Bible Commentary on the New English Bible. 1975.

Williams, A. L. *Joel and Amos. The Minor Prophets Unfolded*. 1918.

Wolff, H. W. *Joel and Amos*. Hermeneia. 1977.

Obadiah
The Prophet of God's Sovereignty

Prophetic oracles against foreign nations, though full of the language of doom, are also implicitly messages of hope for God's people. Such oracles look forward to a time when the predicted demise of the nation under attack will open the way for the restored, purified Israel to blossom once again as the flower of all God's plantings. Obadiah's message fits this pattern and in some ways even typifies it.[6]

—*Douglas Stuart, OT scholar*

1. Date

The date is uncertain since no specific date is mentioned in the text itself and the circumstances discussed in reference to the calamity of Jerusalem (vss. 10-14) are difficult to pinpoint. However there are three possibilities: (1) around 850 BC after the capture and plundering of Jerusalem by the Philistines and Arabians in the reign of Jehoram; (2) around 597 BC after the destruction of Jerusalem by Nebuchadnezzar; or (3) around 400 BC after the community of Judah was reestablished.

Douglas Stuart makes a good case for the second date, noting, "It is the exilic period, particularly the early exile (580s or shortly thereafter) that meets the criterion best. Most importantly, four other OT passages from the same early sixth-century period reflect the same sort of situation and perspective found in Obadiah: Ps. 137:7; Lam. 4:18-22; Ezek. 25:12-14; 35:1-15."[7] However few commentators are dogmatic as to a time of origin. Peter C. Craigie writes, "Proposals with respect to the book's date have ranged from as early as the ninth century BC to as late as the fifth century BC. With such disparity, it is clear that the internal evidence of the book, upon which hypotheses of date must be constructed, is thoroughly ambivalent."[8]

2. Location: Israel/Judah

3. Purpose
   This book is not so much a warning to Edom, as it is a consolation to Israel. The contrast is made between Edom, which would completely fall, and the house of Jacob which would remain. In the final outcome, Yahweh would rule all nations from Zion.

4. Theme: The destruction of Edom and the restoration of Israel.

5. Meaning of Name
   This book is entitled *Obade Yah* which means "servant of Yahweh." The Septuagint entitled this book, *Obdiou*; and Jerome's Vulgate gives it the title, *Abdias*.

6. Audience: Written to the Israelites concerning the nation of Edom.

7. Outline

> I. The Destruction of Edom, 1-16
> II. The Restoration of Israel, 17-21

8. Memory Work

Obadiah 3
*The pride of your heart has
   deceived you,
you who live in the clefts of the
   rock,
whose dwelling is high,
   who say in your heart,
"Who will bring me down to the
   ground?"*

Obadiah 15
*For the day of the Lord is near upon
   all the nations
As you have done, it shall be done
   to you,
your deeds shall return on your
   own head.*

9. Special Notes

A. Destruction: The book of Obadiah has often been criticized as being narrowly nationalistic and retributive in its spirit. It seems to desire the exaltation of the Jews at the cost of the people of Edom. We must remember that God did not destroy Edom because of the hatred that existed between that nation and Israel; rather, destruction came because of God's holiness and justice toward sin.

B. Length: Obadiah is the shortest book in the Old Testament.

C. There is a definite correlation between Obadiah 1-6 and Jeremiah 49:9-16. Who borrowed from whom? This depends on how you date the book of Obadiah. Scholars who date Obadiah in the ninth century assign it priority over Jeremiah 49. Those who date it in the fifth century see Obadiah borrowing from Jeremiah. Some scholars have chosen a middle position inventing a third source from which both prophets borrowed. Since we cannot date Obadiah with any certainty, it is useless to hold dogmatically to any point here. Stuart has written, "It must be admitted that we simply do not possess enough information to be able to settle certain issues about Obadiah and must therefore hold many positions tentatively."[9]

D. The book of Obadiah is a prophecy against one of the enemies of Israel. Many of Israel's prophets prophesied against her enemies. To put this in perspective, consider Douglas Stuart's chart, which lists the nations surrounding Israel and the prophetic utterances against those nations.

Prophetic Oracles Against Foreign Nations[10]

Major Prophets	Minor Prophets	Short/Incidental
Against Assyria:		
Isa. 10:15-19	Mic. 5:5 6	Jonah 3:4
Isa. 14:24-27	Nahum	Zech. 10:11
Isa. 37:21-35	Zeph. 2:13-15	Isa. 10:25
		Isa. 30:31
Against Ammon:		
Jer. 49:1-6	Amos 1:13-15	Isa. 11:14
Ezek. 25:1-7	Zeph. 2:8-11	Jer. 25:21
	(with Moab)	
Against Arabia:		
Isa. 21:13-17		Jer. 25:24
Jer. 49:28-32 (with Hazor)		
Against Aram Damascus:		
Isa. 17	Amos 1:3-5	Isa. 7:7-8
Jer. 49:23-27	Zech. 9:1-2	Isa. 8:4

Major Prophets	Minor Prophets	Short/Incidental
Against Babylon:		
Isa. 13:1-22; Isa. 47	Hab. 2:4-20	
Isa. 14:3-23		
Isa. 21:1-10		
Jer. 50, 51		
Against Cush:		
Isa. 18	Zeph. 2:12	
Isa. 20 (with Egypt)		
Against Edom:		
Isa. 21:11-12	Amos 1:11-12	Joel 3:19
Jer. 49:7-22	Obadiah	Isa. 11:14
Ezek. 35	Mal. 1:2-5	Jer. 25:21
Ezek. 25:12-14		Lam. 4:21
Against Egypt:		
Isa. 19		Joel 3:19
Isa. 20 (with Cush)		Zech. 10:10-11
Jer. 46		Zech. 14:18-19
Ezek. 29, 30, 31, 32		
Against Elam:		
Jer. 49:34-39		
Against Moab:		
Isa. 15, 16	Amos 2:1 3	Isa. 11:14
Jer. 48	Zeph. 2:8-11;	Jer. 25:21
Ezek. 25:8-11	(with Ammon)	
Against Philistia:		
Isa. 14:28-32	Amos 1:6-8	Obad. 19
Jer. 47	Zeph. 2:4-7	Isa. 11:14
Ezek. 25:15-17	Zech. 9:2-8	Jer 25:20

Major Prophets	Minor Prophets	Short/Incidental

Against Tyre (and Sidon):

Isa. 23 (with Sidon)		
Ezek. 26, 27	Joel 4:4-8	Jer 25:22 (with Sidon)
Ezek. 28	Amos 1:9-10	
(vss. 20-23 with Sidon)		

Against the Nations in general:

Isa. 10:12-14	Joel 4:9-16
Isa. 24	Mic. 7:8-17
Isa. 34	Hag. 2:20-22
Isa. 63:1-16	Zeph. 1:2-3
Jer. 25:15-38	Zech. 12:1-9
Ezek 38, 39	Zech 14:12-19

9. Special Notes

The book of Obadiah is concerned with the nation of Edom. To understand Obadiah we have to understand the history of Edom and Israel. Edom means "red" or "ruddy." Edom was the name given to the territory south of the Dead Sea on both sides of the Wadi Arabah. This land had a particular reddish color in the soil due to the sandstone of the district. Today Edom is the territory that makes up the southern part of the kingdom of Jordan. Although it is bordered to the east by desert, rainfall in the plateaus makes farming possible.

Edom was a descendent of Esau (Gen. 36:1, 8) the older twin brother of Jacob. The Scriptures predict that the descendants of Esau and Jacob would have conflict. History has proven the Bible to be true on this point.

Archaeological digs have discovered evidence of occupation in the eastern region of Edom that dates back at least five thousand years. Archaeologists say that Edom was settled and had developed a monarchy before Israel. Edom prohibited Moses and the children of Israel from passing through its territory on the journey out of Egypt (Num. 20:14-21). Edom was a strategically important area in ancient Palestine because of the King's Highway (Num. 20:17), which ran through the eastern section of Edom connecting Egypt with ancient Mesopotamia.

Historically, Edom and Israel were always at odds. Early in the monarchy of Israel, Saul fought successfully against the Edomites gaining control of Edom (I Sam. 14:47). David's conquest was particularly bloody as he instituted the holy ban against the males of Edom and established a permanent army in its territory (I Kings 11:15-17; II Sam. 8:13-14). During Solomon's reign he was able to control the land of Edom and use the port of Ezion-geber to receive materials for his building projects (I Kings 9:26).

During the reign of Jehoshaphat (c. 874-850 BC), Judah controlled Edom and also used the port of Ezion-geber (I Kings 22:47-49). Between 849 and 842 BC the Edomites were able to escape the rule of Israel during the reign of Jehoram. They set up a king of their own and maintained their independence for fifty or sixty years (II Kings 8:20-22). Between 800 and 785 BC, King Uzziah recaptured Edom and built the city of Elath in her territory. During the time of Ahaz (c. 734 BC) the Edomites again rose to power and defeated Judah reclaiming its territory and the city of Elath (II Kings 16:6). From this time onward Judah was unable to exercise control over Edom. Edom fell to the Assyrians in 732 BC and continued to be a vassal of the Assyrian empire until Assyria fell to the Babylonians in the late seventh century.

When Nebuchadnezzar conquered Assyria, he demanded loyalty from the Edomites and the other nations of the Syria-Palestine territory. Edom attended the conference of King Zedekiah of Judah when he attempted to unite surrounding nations against the Babylonians. When King Zedekiah finally revolted against the Babylonians, Edom joined with the Babylonians to help squash the revolt. The Jews would not easily forget how Edom helped in their defeat. When the Jews were deported to Babylon, it left the Edomites free to inhabit the abandoned land of Judah. They occupied the land of Hebron, which later became Idumea.

During the fourth century BC, the Edomite land was invaded by a group of Arabs known as the Nabateans. This lead to a greater migration of Edomites into Idumea (once the territory of Judah). When the Maccabean wars for Jewish independence were fought in the second century BC, Jewish armies gained control of Idumea and forced its inhabitants to convert to Judaism. Thus the writings of Obadiah were fulfilled, "For the violence done to your brother Jacob, shame shall cover you, and you shall be cut off forever" (Ob. 10).

Although the Idumeans were forced to convert to Judaism, the Jerusalem Jews never really accepted them. They still considered them to be Edomites. In the New Testament, King Herod the Great was an Idumean. Although he proclaimed himself to be the "King of the Jews," the Jews never accepted him as king. They considered him an Edomite, and therefore, an enemy of Israel.

11. The Person

"The vision of Obadiah" is the title contained in the first line of this book. About a dozen men in the Old Testament, none of whom are related or identified with this prophet, share the name *Obade-Yah*. Obadiah thought of himself as a prophet, and he ascribed his words to God (vss. 1, 4, 8, 18). We have no information about him in his book or in parallel passages in the Old Testament. As Peter C. Craigie has noted, "His message was preserved, but the medium remains unknown."[11]

12. The Call: Besides the inscription in his book, we have no information as to the call of Obadiah.

13. Structure and Form

The book is a prophetic oracle written in poetic form. It follows the typical pattern for an oracle against a foreign power. We can surmise that Obadiah was familiar with this style of oratory because he used it so effectively.

14. Theology

Israel and Edom had a long history of animosity before Obadiah ever penned his book. Was the book written with a vindictive voice? Was Obadiah seeking retribution from one of Israel's most hated enemies?

No love existed between Israel and Edom. In an attempt to win favor with the Babylonians, Edom betrayed Israel. Obadiah writes, "For the violence done to your brother Jacob, shame shall cover you, and you shall be cut off forever"(vs. 10). The Jews believed that the Edomites helped the Babylonians to burn down the temple of Jerusalem. Israel had every reason to hate the Edomites.

The Law taught that God would take care of Israel's enemies. This is the central theological teaching of Obadiah. God would punish the enemies of Israel and exalt Israel above every nation on earth. Why would God do this? In the Semitic mind, the power of a country represented the power of its God. As God exalted Israel, he himself would be exalted. All the nations would take notice of the power of Israel and see that her God was powerful. Ultimately, God was claiming Edom as his own. He ruled her as he ruled every nation on the earth. If a nation did not see for themselves that God was the Sovereign God and honor him, then they would be forced to acknowledge him. Obadiah 21 reads, "Saviors shall go up to Mount Zion to rule Mount Esau; and the kingdom shall be the Lord's." God was going to crush Edom. But why? So that Edom and all the surrounding nations would know that he was king.

Do we believe that God is sovereign? In times of trouble and distress do we trust that he will deliver us from calamity? Do we trust that God will vindicate us before our enemies? God is sovereign over all the land. We must put our trust and confidence in him and in him alone.

15. Messianic Expectations

The last verse in Obadiah mentions the kingdom of the Lord. Obadiah carries a larger theological picture than just the conquest of Edom. God is king, and his kingdom will advance in the world. No enemy will stall God's march. Power belongs to God, and he will reign over all the earth.

References

Allen, L. *The Books of Joel, Obadiah, Jonah and Micah*. New International Commentary on the Old Testament. 1976.

Baker, D., D. Alexander and B. Waltke. *Obadiah, Jonah, Micah*. Tyndale Old Testament Commentary. 1988.

Bewer, J. A. A *Critical and Exegetical Commentary on Obadiah and Joel*. International Critical Commentary. 1911.

Coggins, R. J. and S. P. Re'emi. *Nahum, Obadiah, Esther*. International Theological Commentary. 1985.

Eaton, J. H. *Obadiah, Nahum, Habakkuk, Zephaniah*. Torch Bible Commentaries. 1961.

Lanchester, H. C. O. *Obadiah and Jonah*. 1918.

Mason, R. *Micah, Nahum, Obadiah*. 1991.

Peckham, G. A. *An Introduction to the Study of Obadiah*. 1910.

Wade, G. W. *The Books of the Prophets Micah, Obadiah, Joel and Jonah*. Westminster Commentaries. 1925.

Watts, J. D. W. *The Books of Joel, Obadiah, Jonah, Nahum, Habakkuk and Zephaniah*. The Cambridge Bible Commentary on the New English Bible. 1975.

_____. *Obadiah: A Critical and Exegetical Commentary*. 1969.

SECTION TWO

The Eighth Century Prophets of the Assyrian Period

Amos
The Prophet of Social Justice

Jonah Ben Amittai
The Prophet of God's Universal Love

Hosea Ben Beeri
The Prophet of Unconditional Love

Isaiah Ben Amoz
The Prophet of Holiness

Micah of Moresheth
The Prophet of the Poor

The Eighth Century Prophets

Meaning of Name	Approx. Date	Prophesied to	Message
Amos			
"Burden-bearer"	786-742	Israel	Samaria must fall because of her sins
Jonah			
"Dove"	780-740	Nineveh	Universality of God's love
Hosea			
"Salvation"	750-715	Israel	Idoatry and God's unconditional love
Isaiah			
"Yahweh is Salvation"	742-698	Judah	Salvation is by God's gift
Micah			
"Who is Yahweh?"	740-710	Judah	Obey God from a trusting heart

Joel 2:12–13
But let justice roll on like a river,
   righteousness like a never-failing
      stream.

Jonah 4:26
I knew that you are a gracious and compassionate
   God, slow to anger and abounding in love.

Hosea 6:6
For I desire mercy not sacrifice,
   and acknowledgement of God
rather than burnt
   offerings.

Isaiah 1:16-17
Take your evil deeds
   out of my sight!
Stop doing wrong;
   learn to do right!
Seek justice;
   encourage the oppressed.
Defend the cause of the fatherless,
   plead the case of the widow.

Micah 6:8
He has showed you, O man, what is
   good,
and what does the Lord require
   of you?
To act justly and to love mercy
   and to walk humbly with your
      God.

Were these things real? Did I see those brave and noble countrymen of mine laid low in death and weltering in their blood? Did I see our country laid waste and in ruins? Did I see soldiers marching, the earth trembling and jarring beneath their measured tread? Did I see the ruins of smoldering cities and deserted homes? Did I see the flag of my country, that I had followed so long, furled to be no more unfurled forever? Surely they are but the vagaries of mine own imagination.... But hush! I now hear the approach of battle, that low, rumbling sound in the West is the roar of cannon in the distance.

—Sam Watkins, (writing on his experience as a private in the Civil War from my hometown of Columbia, Tennessee.)

Amos
The Prophet of Social Justice

But let justice roll on like a river;
righteousness like a never-failing stream.
—Amos 5:24

It is not easy for men to stand aside and form a fair judgment on the community in which they have been brought up, and even when they realize that things are wrong, they are apt to be oppressed by the knowledge that they cannot escape from personal complicity. This is emphatically not true of Amos.
—*Theodoare H. Robinson, OT scholar*

1. Date

According to Amos 1:1, Amos prophesied during the days of Uzziah, king of Judah (783-742) and Jeroboam II king of Israel (786-746). The book focuses on one great message, which Amos delivered about 750 BC.

2. Location

Bethel and Gilgal in the Northern Kingdom of Israel. Bethel at this time was the most important shrine of Yahweh in Samaria. In Bethel, Jacob once heard a divine voice, "The land on which you lie I will give to you and to your descendants" (Gen. 28:13). At Bethel, Jeroboam I set up a cult for Yahweh who had "brought Israel out of the land of Egypt" (I Kings 12:28). After the exodus from Egypt, the Jews first entered into the land of promise at Gilgal. Here Joshua gave his word, "A living God is among you, he will without fail drive out the Canaanites for your sake" (Josh. 3:10). Bethel and Gilgal were the two places where the time-hallowed worship of Yahweh was most sacred.

3. Purpose

Amos prophesied concerning Israel's accountability to the Sovereign Lord for her gross violation of his holy covenant. God did not accept the sham and pretense of empty formalism in worship and community life. Instead, he demanded genuine justice and national righteousness (Amos 5:24).

4. Theme: Israel must fall because of her sinfulness.

5. Meaning of Name: Burden-bearer.

6. Audience: Israel, the Northern Kingdom.

7. Outline of Amos

I. God's punishment is in store for neighboring nations, Judah and Israel, Chapters 1-2

II. Israel's wrongs and God's warnings, Chapters 3-6

III. Five visions of Israel's doom, Chapters 7-9
   A. Vision 1: Locusts, 7:1-3

B. Vision 2: Fire, 7:4-6
C. Vision 3: The plumb line, 7:7-9
D. Parenthesis: Amos' encounter with Amaziah, 7:10-17
E. Vision 4: The basket of summer fruit, 8:1-14
F. Vision 5: The smitten sanctuary, 9:1-10

IV. Epilogue: Glimpses of hope beyond the doom, 9:11-15

8. Memory Work

Amos 3:2
You only have I chosen
  of all the families of the earth;
therefore I will punish you
  for all your sins (NIV).

Amos 3:7-8
Surely the Sovereign Lord does
  nothing
without revealing his plan
  to his servants the prophets.

The lion has roared—
  who will not fear?
The Sovereign Lord has spoken—
  who can but prophesy? (NIV).

Amos 5:18-20
Woe to you, who long
  for the day of the Lord!
Why do you long for the day of the
  Lord?
That day will be darkness, not
  light.

It will be as though a man fled from
  a lion
  only to meet a bear,
as though he entered his house
  and rested his hand on the wall
  only to have a snake bite him.
Will not the day of the Lord be
  darkness, not light—
pitch-dark, without a ray of
  brightness? (NIV).

Amos 5:24
But let justice roll on like a river,
  righteousness like a never-failing stream!
  (NIV).

9. Special Notes

A. The day of Yahweh (The day of the Lord; the *Yom Yahweh*): Amos' hearers anticipated that the coming day of Yahweh would be a day of national victory. Amos informed them instead that it would be a day of national ruin because of their sins (5:18-20).

B. Vision: Amos speaks of his call in terms of five visions, which God showed him concerning the destruction of the Northern Kingdom.

C. Style: Amos is called the "prophet of social justice," because of his burning condemnation of oppression. Amos is a master of a clear, forceful Hebrew style. He uses parallelism and word play, as well as other stylistic devices to drive home his intense message to his hearers.

D. Amos' indictments against God's people:
  i.   The extravagance of the rich, 3:15
  ii. The self-indulgence of the gluttonous women, 4:1
  iii. The perversion of justice, 5:10, 12; 6:12-14

iv.   The complacency of Zion, 6:1-6
v.   The amassing of fortunes by force and fraud, 5:11-12
vi.   The advancement of business by cheating, 8:15
vii. The enslavement of people, 8:6
viii. The worship of false gods, 5:5; 8:14

E. In Amos we see for the first time the words of a Hebrew prophet recorded and passed down as an individual text. Certain events in the lives of other prophets were recorded, (e.g., Nathan, Elijah and Elisha), but Amos' words are collected into a type of anthology. James D. Newsome, Jr., a professor at Columbia Theological Seminary, has noted:

> In the case of Amos an effort is made to preserve the words of the prophet in the very literary forms in which they were originally uttered. It is the first step in the long process, which ultimately leads to the inclusion of the book of Amos in the canon of the Old Testament and, beyond that, to the whole phenomenon of a corpus of prophetic writings. It should be emphasized that the focus of this literary activity is upon the prophetic message.[12]

We do not know the reason why this new process was started; but it soon became the norm, and other collections were added to this important collection.

F. Apart from Jonah, Amos was the only prophet sent from one country to another country to prophesy. Amos faced the added danger of being sent from the southern nation of Judah to preach to Israel in the north.

10. Historical Context

When people read the prophets they generally make two mistakes: They read them as novels, and they read them without any historical context. For a prophetic message to be understood, it must be placed within its historical setting. The theological term for this is *Sitz im Leben*—setting in life. For Amos, there are four nations that need to be considered: Assyria, Syria, Israel and Judah.

As early as the twelfth century BC, Tiglath-Pileser I, the lion of Assyria, tried to overtake the nation of Israel. His forces moved as far as the mountains of Lebanon before they had to return home because of a lack of clear political and military planning. From Adad-nirari II (909-889 BC) onwards, the kings of Assyria became more interested in acquiring extensive territories in the surrounding countries. From 858-824, Shalmaneser III came to the throne and continued Assyrian expansion and imperialism. In 853 BC, Shalmaneser III fought a coalition of Syrian minor princes who were led by Ben-Hadad of Damascus and Ahab of Israel in the Battle of Qarqar. Assyria lost this battle, but they fought again on Mt. Hermon in 841 BC and won, taking Syria captive and forcing Jehu of Israel to pay tribute. Shalmaneser III was succeeded by Adad-narari III (811-784 BC) who continued the Assyrian domination by completely crushing Damascus in Syria and by extracting tribute from Israel.

After Adad-nirari III, the Assyrian kingdom fell into weakness for the next fifty years. This was partially due to the resurgence of the Babylonian empire and also because of a lack of leadership for the Assyrians. This time of weakness gave Syria and Israel a chance for renewal and prosperity. John Bright, author of *A History of Israel*, comments:

> The eighth century brought a dramatic reversal of fortune, which projected Israel and Judah to heights of power and prosperity unknown since David and Solomon. This was due partly to the fact that both states were blessed with able rulers. But the chief reason lay in a happy turn of events of which Israel became the beneficiary.[13]

This time of prosperity was short lived, and the Assyrian kingdom was to rise to great power once again.

When Tiglath-Pileser III (745-727 BC) came to power in Assyria, he determined to make the nation of Assyria the controlling force in the region. J. Alberto Soggin, an OT professor, writes of him, stating, "After the start made by his predecessors, it was his lot to lead the Neo-Assyrian Empire to the pinnacle of power and to bring it to its completion in concept and system if not in territory."[14] Tiglath-Pileser III expanded westward, ultimately taking Israel as a vassal territory. When Tiglath-Pileser took Israel, he replaced the Israelite king Pekah with his own vassal Hoshea. With the death of Tiglath-Pileser III in 727 BC, neither Ben-Hadad of Damascus nor Hoshea of Israel wished to cause trouble for the nation of Assyria. It was not long, however, 724 BC, before Hoshea, supported by the promises of Egypt, decided to challenge the new Assyrian throne.

The new Assyrian king, Shalmaneser V, was prepared to meet Hoshea's rebellion, and he proceeded to answer the Israelite uprising. Soggin remarks:

> What had to come, came without delay. Shalmaneser V did not hesitate to suppress with violence the movement directed against him...Samaria was able to hold out for about two more years against the Assyrian siege. It was not until the death of Shalmaneser V and the beginning of the reign of Sargon II that the city succumbed to the Assyrian onslaught."[15]

Such was the death of the great nation of Israel. The Southern Kingdom, Judah, was able to escape extermination, but their day of judgment was still to come.

The prophet Amos prophesied during the period of Assyrian weakness between the reigns of Adad-nirari III and Tilglath-Pileser III. This was a time of great prosperity for both Israel and Judah. Jehoash (804-788) and Jeroboam II were able to secure supremacy for Israel in Northern Israel and Syria. This age has been called "the Victorian Age of the Hebrew kingdoms."[16] Jeroboam II extended the boundary of Israel and created revenue by placing customhouses at every port and every mountain post of his region. The natural trade route controlled by Israel brought both merchants and money to the capital city, Samaria. The rich began to become more and more hungry for increased wealth and power. The rising upper classes began to disregard and then to abuse the common man. Norman Snaith, an OT scholar and professor, characterizes this period by writing:

> We have, therefore, a country with great scarcity and poverty in the midst of plenty, a state of society in which the rich grow steadily richer and more luxurious in their tastes, whilst the poor become even poorer until they lack even the necessities of life. The country was ripe for civil strife.[17]

It was into such a civil and social crises that Yahweh called Amos to prophesy. Amos was commissioned to take an unwanted and unpopular message to an unsympathetic and uncaring audience.

11. The Person

The name Amos means "burden-bearer," or it could be shortened to mean "borne by God." It is derived from a Hebrew verb meaning "to lift a burden" or "to carry."[18]

Amos lived in the town of Tekoa. Some scholars locate Tekoa around five miles south of Bethlehem, and others place the town twelve miles south of Jerusalem. Some avoid giving a direct location of the town by simply assigning its location to the region of Southern Judah.[19] William R. Harper, author of an excellent commentary on Amos and Hosea, clears up the matter:

> The place lies six miles south of Bethlehem (twelve miles south of Jerusalem). The hill, four or five acres, is broad at the top and not steep. The surrounding country is sterile and rocky, but rich in pasturage. The wilderness of Tekoa is part of the wilderness of Judah.[20]

It is upon this hill of Tekoa that Amos lived and worked.

A modern, Palestinian town of Tekoa exists today. When my family lived in Jerusalem, we often led a church service in Bethlehem. One family came from Tekoa to Bethlehem to attend the service. I always felt a special affinity toward this family because I knew they were from Amos' village of Tekoa. Like Amos, they were farmers.

Amos was a shepherd and a keeper of sycamore fig trees. As a shepherd, Amos raised a special breed of small sheep with stunted growth that were prized for their wool. It is possible that the reference in Amos 7:14 means that Amos was also a cattle herdsman.

What was a keeper of sycamore fig trees? The sycamore, a wild fig tree, needed to be nipped or cut at the tip in order to allow its sap to run. If it was nipped at the proper time, then an edible fruit would be produced, which the lower classes could afford to buy. Some have attempted to twist the words of Amos' profession around to prove that he was a cultic functionary in Tekoa. But Amos was a simple shepherd and keeper of sycamore trees. John D.E.W. Watts, an author and scholar, comments:

> The picture of Amos as a rough countryman, practicing trades normal to the life of a small village like that of Tekoa, remains the best explanation of these terms and the most fitting background for an understanding of the prophet himself.[21]

Amos was an ordinary man. Yet God took this shepherd and sycamore fig tree pincher and made him the great prophet of social justice.

Amos was the first of the literary prophets to experience what would become commonplace among the prophets—persecution. We do not know what type of reaction his message received from the common people at Bethel, but the reception by the religious leaders was not cordial. Amaziah the priest of Bethel demonstrated this hostility when he sought a royal commission to expel Amos from the land (Amos 7:10-13). Amaziah rebuked Amos to his face commanding him to go back south to Judah to prophesy doom to his own people. Amos responded to Amaziah by repeating his prophetic call and declaring that his message, although unpleasant, was God's message and not his own (Amos 7:14-17).

12. The Call

What changed this country shepherd into the great eighth-century prophet of social reform? Amos himself attributes the change to his call. Amos' call was not an elaborate one, but it did point to the nature of his mission. Amos 7:10-15 records the dramatic encounter between Amos of Tekoa and Amaziah, the chief priest of the temple of Bethel. Amaziah saw Amos as a southern visionary (*hozeh*) who earned his living by seeking compensation for his prophetic oracles. This placed him in the tradition of Samuel and other early prophets (I Sam. 9:8; I Kings 14:2-3; II Kings 8:8). Amaziah warned Amos to return to Judah in order to peddle his prophetic wares on his own people. Amos responded:

> *I am not a prophet* (nabi), *and I am not a prophet's disciple.*
> *I am a cattle breeder and a tender of sycamore figs. But*
> *the Lord took me away from following the flock, and the*
> *Lord said to me, "Go, prophesy to my people Israel."*
> —Amos 7:14-15, (*Tanakh*)

Here Amos states that he is not a cultic prophet, but he prophesies because he is Yahweh-commissioned. His call came directly and also unexpectedly from Yahweh.

Amos regarded himself as one who walked with God. In Amos 3:3-9, Amos asks who could possibly reject God's call?

Do two walk together
unless they have agreed to do so?
Does a lion roar in the thicket
when he has no prey?
Does he growl in his den
when he has caught nothing?
Does a bird fall into a trap on the ground
where no snare has been set?
Does a trap spring up from the earth
when there is nothing to catch?
When a trumpet sounds in a city,
do not the people tremble?
When disaster comes to a city,
has not the Lord caused it?

Surely the Sovereign Lord does
nothing
without revealing his plan
to his servants the prophets.
The lion has roared—
who will not fear?
The Sovereign Lord has spoken—
who can but prophesy? (NIV).

These verses also demonstrate the intimacy of Amos' relationship with God. Commenting on these verses, Abraham J. Heschel, author of *The Prophets*, writes,

These lines suggest a relation of intimacy, characteristic of those who are in close contact with one another and who have opened their hearts and their minds to such a degree that they deeply know and understand one another. Intimacy, however, never becomes familiarity. God is Lord, and the prophets are his servants."[22]

In the book of Amos, Amos presented himself as a person who had been changed by the presence of God. He was driven by Yahweh to take this disruptive presence to the nation of Israel.

13. Structure and Form

The language of Amos is not that of an unschooled herdsman. George W. Anderson, a professor of the Old Testament, comments, "The powerful effect of his words is the result not only of profound conviction but also of literary skill."[23] Amos displays a brilliant use of figures and allusions in his oracles. By studying these, one can deduce that Amos was alert to the situation around him. He knew the lowliness of the poor (2:6-7, 8:4-6); he was acquainted with the luxury of the rich (3:15, 4:1, 6:4-7); he was familiar with the political struggles around him (1:3-2:3); he knew about the cultic centers of the North (4:5, 5:21ff., 7:10-17). All of these references point to the genius of this prophet who gave himself to worship and opened himself up to God's wisdom.

The book of Amos is easily outlined into memorable categories:

Chapters one and two present a collection of oracles of judgment against the nations. The oracles pronounce the transgressions of the nation and then the punishment they can expect.

Chapters three through six are a collection of three sermons. Each sermon begins with the phrase, "Hear this word." The first sermon addresses the topic of the privileges and responsibilities of election; the second sermon speaks to Israel's luxurious excesses and vain piety; the third sermon announces the horror and finality of Israel's coming punishment.

Chapters seven, eight, and nine consist of a series of five visions, each with an interpreting oracle, and a closing epilogue. Through the medium of oracle, sermon and vision, Amos presents Yahweh's Word to the people of Israel.

14. Theology

A. The Universal Sovereignty of God.

The book of Amos declares the universal sovereignty of God.

Yahweh rules over the cosmos and everything in it. Although the gods of Canaan claimed to control the forces of nature, Yahweh, the God of Israel, was the real moving force behind the cycle of nature. He was the one who caused the sun to rise and set. Yahweh brought rain in time of drought and produced fruit for the harvest.

God allowed nations to rise and fall according to his purpose. He controlled the destiny of Israel's neighbors and the destiny of Israel herself. In Amos 1:3-2:3, Amos pronounced judgment against Israel's neighbors. Because of their sins, God would punish Syria, Philistia, Tyre, Ammon and Moab. But then Amos brought a new twist into his oracle of doom: God would not only judge her neighbors, but his eye was turned toward Israel as well. The same punishment that God used against the nations would be used on Israel.

God is sovereign over the nations, and also sovereign over the individual. Since Yahweh is the Sovereign God, no one can escape his presence. Amos 9:2-3 states:

> *Though they dig down to the depths*
> *of the grave,*
> *from there my hand will take*
> *them.*
> *Though they climb up to the*
> *heavens,*
> *from there I will bring them*
> *down.*
> *Though they hide themselves on the*
> *top of Carmel,*
> *there I will hunt them down and*
> *seize them.*
> *Though they hide from me at the*
> *bottom of the sea,*
> *there I will command the*
> *serpent to bite them (NIV).*

No person and no nation can hide from God. Israel, herself could not hide from God. As God would punish other nations for their sins, so Israel must be judged for her sins. Yahweh is an inescapable judge. His sovereignty is universal.

Brevard S. Childs, author of *Introduction to the Old Testament as Scripture*, sees three hymns scattered throughout the book of Amos. Each of these hymns follows the meter and form of a psalm. They each extol the sovereignty of God. Childs writes, "In their present literary position the hymns serve as a type of commentary—indeed in a liturgical form—which elaborates on the nature of the God of Israel whose threatening appearance in judgment has been announced."[24] The verses of this hymn are found in Amos 4:13; 5:8-9; 9:5-6. Placed together they form the following hymn:

> *He who forms the mountains,*
> *creates the wind,*
> *and reveals his thoughts to man.*
> *He who turns dawn to darkness*
> *and treads the high places of the*
> *earth—*
> *the Lord God Almighty is his*
> *name.*
>
> *He who made the Pleiades and*
> *Orion,*
> *who turns blackness into dawn*
> *and darkens day into night,*
> *who calls for the waters of the sea*
> *and pours them out over the*
> *face of the land—*
> *the Lord is his name.*
> *He flashes destruction on the*
> *stronghold*

and brings the fortified city to
ruin.

The Lord, the Lord Almighty,
he who touches the earth and it
melts,
and all who live in it mourn—
the whole land rises like the Nile,
then sinks like the river of
Egypt—
he who builds his lofty palace in the
heavens
and sets its foundation on the
earth,
who calls for the waters of the sea
and pours them out over the face
of the land—
the Lord is his name (NIV).

Amos recognized the universal sovereignty of Yahweh. He
extolled this characteristic of God in psalms and hymns. He
communicated this idea in his oracles. His desire was for Israel to
recognize this quality in God and for her to respond accordingly.

B. Yahweh Has Entered Into a Special Covenant Relationship
With Israel.

Amos declares in Amos 3:2:

You only have I chosen
of all the families of the earth;
therefore I will punish you
for all your sins (NIV).

Israel enjoyed a unique relationship with God, but with this unique relationship came unique responsibilities. If Israel failed to recognize her special position, then Yahweh would judge her severely.

Although Amos never used the word, Israel's unique relationship with God was established by his covenant. Since God gave Israel the Torah, he expected her to follow his standard of righteousness. Amos views the reason for Israel's national and social corruption as sin. If God's people want to survive, then they must abandon their immorality and injustice and follow the principles of righteousness, justice and holiness as expressed in the Law.

Amos lashed out at Israel because of her moral laxity. She had forgotten God and lost her integrity. Because of this, God became Israel's enemy. George L. Robinson, author of *The Twelve Minor Prophets*, lists the charges that Amos leveled against Israel as follows:

> Wealth and luxury, frivolity and corruption, opulence and oppression, summer and winter palaces, ivory couches, songs of revelry and wine…victimizing the poor, confiscating their garments for debt, unbridled licentiousness even under the cloak of religion, hypocritical tithing, and hollow Sabbath-observance, even pilgrimages to far distant shrines.[25]

Amos' indictment against Israel was harsh and scathing. He deeply realized Israel's need for repentance.

Israel's doctrine of election had blinded the nation—she believed she had a license to sin. The language of Amos is kindred to Paul's in Romans 6. Election does not guarantee pardon. Israel did not choose Yahweh, but Yahweh chose Israel. Election did not mean that God would respond to Israel's every plea: strength in weakness, prosperity in poverty, health in sickness, victory in defeat. Election had conditions, "If you will obey my voice and keep my covenant, you shall be my own possession among all peoples" (Ex. 19:5). God had known Israel of all the families of the earth. To know (*yada*) signifies an intimate relationship. It is the same word used for the sexual relationship (Adam knew Eve). This intimacy required that Israel respond to God in a special way. Election included responsibility.

Amos was critical of the election doctrine, which Israel had developed in the eighth century. In one passage he seems to denounce it altogether. Amos 9:7 reads:

> *"To Me, O Israelites, you are*
> *just like the Ethiopians,"*
> *declares the Lord.*
> *"True, I brought Israel up*
> *from the land of Egypt,*
> *but also the Philistines from Caphtor*
> *and the Arameans from Kir." (Tanakh)*

The Syrians and the Philistines were Israel's most dreaded enemies. Yet God's hand was over these nations in the same way that he was over Israel. He gave them a homeland as he had given Israel a homeland. Amos attacked the notion that Yahweh was Israel's national God who was obligated to respond to her every cry and complaint. God did not serve Israel, but Israel served God.

Amos desired for the nation to return to God's standard of righteousness and justice. People must forget their individual pursuits and remember community. It was not feast and festivals, sacrifices and libations, which gave Israel her relationship with God. Instead God sought moral obedience from his people, and this response was demanded of them if they wished to survive.

C. *Yom Yahweh*—The Day of the Lord Is Not a Day of Hope But a Day of Judgment.

If I were to sum up the message of Amos into one capsule phrase, that phrase would be, "Prepare to meet your God, O Israel!" (Amos 4:12). This phrase was closely associated with the interpretation Amos gave to the *Yom Yahweh*, the day of the Lord. This festive day was celebrated each fall during the covenant festival at the turn of the year. The day of the Lord was hoped to be a day of salvation for the national cult of Israel, but Amos twisted this concept in his usage by giving it an idea of judgment (Amos 5:18-20). The people should no longer hope for the day of Yahweh because it would be the day of Israel's demise. Israel was headed for a rendezvous with God.

Israel had strayed long enough; it was now time for her to face judgment. Her people failed to administer justice in court; bribery was an accepted practice; dishonesty in business was the order of the day; great zeal was hypocritically shown in the religious rituals. For these transgressions and others, Israel was warned by Amos to prepare to meet God. Abraham Heschel comments on the message of Amos and writes, "Amos' primary mission is not to predict, but to exhort and to persuade...Israel has failed to seek God, so He will go out to meet Israel."[26] The people of Israel had become complacent in a society of luxury, but they now must repent of slothfulness because Israel is about to meet God. Gerhard von Rad, in his excellent *Old Testament Theology*, remarks,

> Time and time again, with one calamity after another, famine, drought, failure of harvest, failure in war, and epidemics, Yahweh kept knocking at their door, but they paid no heed (Amos 4:6ff). Now, however, this time of indirect warning was over. Israel must now hold herself in readiness to meet her God in person."[27]

Such is the nature of Amos' message to Israel. It is not a pleasant message it is a message of doom. The message is Yahweh's word; therefore, it had to be spoken, and Amos was the spokesman.

Even with this vehement message of doom, Amos was still hopeful that Israel would repent and return to the Lord. The meaning of repentance (*teshubah*) is "to return to the one who gave you life." Although the situation was grave, there still remained a glimmer of hope. Amos writes:

> *Seek good and not evil so that you may live, and that Yahweh, God of Sabaoth, may really be with you as you claim he is. Hate evil, love good, maintain justice at the city gate, and it may be that Yahweh, God of Sabaoth, will take pity on the remnant of Joseph (Amos 5:14-15, JB).*

Amos confirmed to Israel that today is the day of salvation. Tomorrow might be too late. The only hope for Israel was to repent immediately and seek God.

D. Prophet of Social Justice

The prophet Amos was keenly aware of the social condition of Israel in the seventh century BC. He boldly spoke against the social atrocities occurring around him. In doing this he continued the legacy of Elijah and Elisha who had championed the cause of the poor and the outcast. As his predecessors, Amos stood against the established aristocracy and pleaded the cause of the individual. Amos recognized the rights given to the common person as stated in the Torah. The nation of Israel existed for the good of the individual and not the individual for the good of the state.

One sees the genius of Amos in his oracles against the landed gentry and the unjust judge. His finger was on the pulse of Israelite society. He catalogs a list of grievances that demonstrate how he personally felt about the wrongs being perpetrated against the lower class. He covers every area, from religion to law and from politics to economics. Following is a breakdown of the social ills he recognized:

The Wealthy Merchants:
sold the needy for a pair of sandals (2:6)
devoured the poor, annihilating the poor from the land (8:4)
longed for the end of religious festivals so they could continue

to cheat the poor (8:5)
used dishonest scales (8:5)
sold grain refuse as grain (8:6)
bought the poor for silver, the needy for a pair of sandals
(8:6)

The Wealthy Landowners:
trampled the heads of the poor into the dust of the ground
(2:7)
pushed off the road the humble of the land (2:7)

The Public Leaders:
hoarded plunder and loot in their fortresses (3:10)
imposed a tax on the poor (5:11)
exacted a levy of grain from the poor (5:11)
took bribes (5:12)
put their hope in the nobles of the leading nations (6:1)
laid on ivory beds, lolling on their couches (6:4)
feasted on lambs from the flock and calves from the stalls
(6:4)
hummed songs with the lute thinking themselves musicians
like David (6:5)
drank straight from the wine bottle and anointed themselves with choicest oils (6:6)
were unconcerned about the ruin of Joseph (6:6)
lolled about at festive meals (6:7)
turned the fruit of righteousness to wormwood (6:12)
took pride in military victories (6:13)

The Sophisticated Ladies:
were like the cows of Bashan (4:1)
defrauded the poor (4:1)
robbed the needy (4:1)
said to their husbands, "Bring us some drinks and let us
carouse!"(4:1)

The Judges of the Law Courts:
    sold for silver those whose cause was just (2:6)
    drank in the house of their God wine bought with the fines
    they imposed (2:8)
    turned justice into wormwood (5:7)
    hurled righteousness to the ground (5:7)
    hated the arbiter in the gate (5:10,15)
    detested him whose plea was just (5:10)
    took bribes (5:12)
    subverted in the gate the cause of the needy (5:12)
    turned justice into poison weed (6:12)

The Pious Israelite:
    father and son visited the same cultic prostitute (2:7)
    reclined by every altar on garments taken in pledge (2:8)
    drank in the house of their God wine bought with fines they
    imposed (2:8)
    after transgressing boasted about sacrifices, tithes, thank
    offerings and freewill offerings (4:4-5)

The Religious Functionaries:
    made the Nazirites drink wine (2:12)
    ordered the prophets not to prophesy (2:12)
    turned the fruit of righteousness into wormwood (6:12)

The Religious Shrines:
    posted notices that read, "Come to Bethel and transgress; to
    Gilgal, and transgress even more" (4:4)
    contained images of Sikkuth and Kiyyun and an astral deity
    (5:26)

The Israelite in General:
    committed great outrages in Samaria and oppressed the
    people (3:9)
    were incapable of doing right (3:10)
    were ravaged by famine, drought, blight and mildew,

locusts, pestilence and military defeat but would not return to God (4:6 12)
built houses of hewn stone (5:11)
planted delightful gardens (5:11)
committed many crimes and countless sins (5:12)
were enemies of the righteous (5:12)
caused the prudent man to keep silent because the times were evil (5:13)
were proud (6:8)
belonged to a sinful kingdom (6:8)

God's Reaction:
God ravaged Samaria by famine, drought, blight and mildew, locusts, pestilence and military defeat (4:6-12)
God spurned your festivals (5:21)
God was not appeased by solemn assemblies (5:21)
God did not accept burnt offerings, meal offerings or gifts of fatlings (5:21-22)
God did not hear their hymns or music of their lutes (5:23)
God was disgusted with the sins of Israel (5:23-24)

15. Messianic Expectation

Although Amos sounded a note of sharp warning to the people of Israel, he allowed a ray of light to shine through in the promise that through judgment God would save his people (Amos 9:8-10). Since God loved his people, salvation was his ultimate goal (Amos 9:11-15).

Amos reminded us that God is more concerned about our hearts than our religious celebrations or traditions. He is concerned that we seek justice and righteousness more than sacrifice or assemblies. We must continually examine ourselves, right our wrongs and seek after the Lord.

16. Important Passages

Amos 7:1-3; 4-6; 7-9; 8:1-2; 9:1-2.

The Growth of a Prophet
An Analysis of the Five Visions of Amos

In just six months' time, God took Amos who was just a shepherd/sycamore-fig-tree-pincher and made him into a great prophet of Israel. He used an ordinary man as his instrument. If God could create this drastic change so quickly in Amos, he can do the same for us today. God changes ordinary people into extraordinary people.

I. **Vision 1: The Locusts.** April-May. Amos 7:1-3.

> *This is what the Sovereign Lord showed me: He was preparing swarms of locusts after the king's share had been harvested and just as the second crop was coming up. When they had stripped the land clean, I cried out, "Sovereign Lord, forgive! How can Jacob survive? He is so small!" So the Lord relented.*
> *"This will not happen," the Lord said.*

The scene here is the spring harvest during the months of April and May. The king's harvest has been reaped and stored. The second harvest, which is for the people, is still in the fields. Amos sees God preparing swarms of locusts that will destroy the people's crops. The time for judgment has arrived. Yet Amos gets sentimental about the people and cries out to God for pardon.

Amos knew the sins of the people. Profanity, greed and injustice ran rampant in the land (2:6-8). The women were lazy and apathetic like cows of Bashan lying on ivory couches (4:1-3). The people had grown fat and comfortable off of the labor of the poor and less fortunate (6:1-7). Amos knew that Israel was guilty of rebellion against God and in need of punishment. But he grew sentimental.

He began to think of the smallness of Israel. He reflected on her place in God's design. His heart went out to his countrymen whom God was about to destroy. His emotions overcame his intellect. Consider the following imaginary diatribe between God and Amos:

> God: "Amos, are they guilty?"
> Amos: "Yes, Lord, they are."
> God: "Amos, have I not judged them fairly?"
> Amos: "Yes, Lord, you have."
> God: "Amos, should they be punished?"
> Amos: "Yes."
> God: "Amos, shall I send locusts?"
> Amos: "No, Lord! See how small and helpless they are. Please spare them."

Amos' sentimentality got the best of him. Isn't it great that none of us struggle with sentimentality today? We are all rock-solid, firmly grounded, steady and consistent. Don't we wish!

How often are we unrighteous because of our emotions? We are controlled by moods. Bad days drag into bad weeks and bad weeks into bad months. It's like Shirley MacLaine's character in *Steel Magnolias*, "I'm not crazy! I've just been in a foul mood for forty years."

Notice that God postponed judgment because of Amos' sentimentality. Was it good that punishment was postponed? Not necessarily. It just delayed God's wrath; it did not cancel it. God still carried out his plan for Israel. What happened in the meantime? What happens when a crop is ready for harvest and it remains in the field? It rots. Israel's situation worsened. Amos' emotional response did not spare anyone. Because his judgment was clouded by sentimentality, more people were hurt.

Sentimentalism and emotionalism can keep God from working powerfully in us. I'm reminded of James 4:17, "Anyone, then, who knows the good he ought to do and doesn't do it, sins" (NIV). Our emotions can paralyze us and keep us from doing what is right. Amos teaches a needed lesson—don't be sentimental, be righteous.

II. **Vision Two: The Fire.** July. Amos 7:4-6.

This is what the Sovereign Lord showed me: The Sovereign Lord was calling for judgment by fire; it dried up the great deep and devoured the land.
Then I cried out, "Sovereign Lord, I beg you, stop! How can Jacob survive?
He is so small."
So the Lord relented.
"This will not happen either," the Sovereign Lord said (NIV).

This vision came to Amos during the dog days of summer. God calls for judgment by fire upon the nation of Israel. The fire would be so intense that it would dry up the primeval waters of the great deep and devour the land.

With this vision Amos got even more emphatic. He begged God to stop. The Hebrew language makes it more emphatic demonstrating the passion of Amos, "No! Desist! Stop!" Amos had gone from a sentimental outburst to outright rebellion. He realized that God is right and judgment must come, but Amos was unwilling to see it come. He begs God to postpone the inevitable.

Amos was acting like a little child. God's prophet acting like a child. Have you ever watched a child when they don't get what they want? Take for example, a little boy or girl that wants chewing gum.

What happens when the parents say, "No, no gum today"? When children don't get what they want, they try emotional ploys. They might whine, beg, perform or attempt to cut a deal ("Gum for a kiss, Daddy"). When these ploys don't work, they resort to rebellion. They might sneak into the gum drawer and grab a piece of gum, take it to their room, unwrap it and try to chew it in secret. They go from emotionalism to rebellion.

As adults we can have the same mentality in our relationship with God. We get emotional with God. Then we get rebellious.

We rebel when we know it would be better to submit. At times, our rebellious, emotional side wins out over our submissive, rational side.

Doesn't it seem amazing that one of God's prophets could have a rebellious heart? Yet not so amazing when we consider our own hearts. People say, "I've heard for years that I need to stop smoking, but I've not changed." Others say, "I don't want to change." Others say, "I'll change later, when my life is in a different place." These comments reveal rebellious hearts. Rebellion does not cancel judgment; it just postpones it.

III. **Vision Three: The Plumb Line.** August. Amos 7:7-9.

> *This is what he showed me: The Lord was standing by a wall that had been built true to plumb, with a plumb line in his hand, and the Lord asked me, "What do you see, Amos?"*
>
> *"A plumb line," I replied. Then the Lord said, "Look, I am setting a plumb line among my people Israel; I will spare them no longer.*
>
> > *The high places of Isaac will be destroyed*
> > *and the sanctuaries of Israel will be ruined;*
> > *with my sword I will rise against the house of Jeroboam" (NIV).*

It is now August, the time to repair the fences around the vineyards in Israel. If the walls are left in disrepair, animals are free to come in and steal the fruit. A plumb line is used to see if the walls have been bent out of true by a year of wind, rain and intense heat. The plumb line will not lie. It will check if the wall is true. It will show any need for repair.

This passage details God's patience as he gently worked with Amos to help him accept God's will. I am reminded of the book of Jonah and the lengths to which God went to win Jonah's submission. With Amos God continued his dialogue. Amos had once responded with emotionalism and then with rebellion. Yet God continued to work on him. God knew the value of one human life. He could have found someone else for the task, but he desired Amos. He patiently taught Amos to accept his will.

Through God's patient and careful instruction, Amos learned to submit to the will of God. He saw the plumb line and measured the walls of Israel. The walls were in shambles. They were beyond repair; they needed to be destroyed. When Israel was held next to God's standard, her sin was easily visible. Amos has no choice but to accept God's standard and respect his judgment.

Amos repented because God patiently worked with him until he accepted the standard. This is exactly what we need in our lives. We need someone to carefully and lovingly hold the plumb line next to our lives so we can see the truth. The plumb line shows us God's standard. Our emotions and our rebellious attitude do not change the truth. We need to repent and accept the truth as God has stated it.

IV. Vision Four: A Basket of Ripe Fruit. Sept. Amos 8:1-2.

> This is what the Sovereign Lord showed me: a basket of
> ripe fruit.
> "What do you see, Amos?" he asked.
> "A basket of ripe fruit," I answered.
> Then the Lord said to me, "The time is ripe for my people
> Israel; I will spare them no longer" (NIV).

September was the month of the fall harvest. When the fruit became ripe, it needed to be harvested immediately. If anyone knew this, Amos did. After all, he was a gardener. When the fruit was not harvested on time, it would rot. The harvest could not be delayed.

In the same way God demonstrated to Amos that his harvest of the nation of Israel could no longer be delayed. God already had postponed judgment for Amos' sake twice. To postpone any longer would only promote further decay in Israel. The time had come. God would delay no longer.

God worked with Amos to deepen Amos' convictions. God could do this because he had a relationship with Amos. He worked through that relationship to take Amos to a deeper level of conviction. Amos had emotionally protested against God's plan to punish Israel. He then went from an emotional protest to outright rebellion against God's plan. But God was patient. He worked with Amos as he worked with the nation of Israel. God attempted to teach Amos his ways, to deepen his convictions, to get Amos to see things from his perspective.

God used an image, with which Amos would have been personally familiar—the image of the harvest (a basket of ripe fruit). He allowed that image to speak to Amos and to teach him. He was interested in his prophet. He wanted his prophet to understand him and to be united with him. God did not run roughshod over Amos, treating him as some mindless instrument. He was sensitive to his humanity and lovingly drew Amos over to his purpose. As with Jonah and Jeremiah, in Amos we see a prophet whom God wooed and coaxed until Amos developed deep, godly convictions.

We too must become people of deep conviction. God desires for us to think like him and act like him. He is always willing to go the extra mile to deepen our convictions. To deepen our convictions, we must deepen our relationship with God. God begins with relationship. He worked with Amos as a father works with his son. He communicated with Amos. He appealed to his sense of rightness. God is also willing to work with us to deepen our relationship with him. As we deepen our relationship with him, our convictions get stronger.

There must be something that drives us to a deeper relationship with God. For Amos it was a basket of fruit, which reminded him of his past and everything he knew about the proper time for harvest. For us it might be a favorite scripture, a close brother or sister, a sermon we love or a specific and meaningful prayer. Our desire is to be deeply spiritual. The secret of Jesus' conviction was his relationship with God. He walked closely with the Father every single day. He had his special place of prayer and special time of prayer. If Jesus needed this time with God, then certainly we do.

Sometimes we need a spiritual wake-up call to remind us of the importance of our relationship with God. In the fall of 1862 the United States of America was in the throes of the most turbulent and costly war of her history. The Confederates under the leadership of General Robert E. Lee were getting the best of the North. Abraham Lincoln knew that he had to do something to unite the Northern cause. The little uprising in South Carolina had grown into a full-scale war and the North was getting tired of fighting. Lincoln pulled out of his desk a speech he had prepared months earlier. This "Emancipation Proclamation" redefined the terms of the War Between the States. No longer was it a war to be fought for federal rights or states rights. It was now a war for freedom and equality for everyone. Lincoln's guess was right. His "Emancipation Proclamation" was the catalyst the North needed to get focused and win the war. Lincoln found a way to deepen the conviction of the Union forces by making the Civil War a war for human freedom. It was their wake-up call.

Amos needed a wake-up call. At times, we all need a spiritual wake-up call. We need to deepen our relationship with God. As our relationship with God deepens, our convictions also deepen. We get stronger. We wake up moody so we get into the Word and God speaks to us until the moods are gone. Things are bad on the job so we pray to the Father until we find the strength to face the bad and wait for the good. Someone disappoints us and we despair, until we talk to a friend and God works through that friend to reinforce our ideals of what friendship is really all about.

Convictions are important. God taught this lesson to Amos. They see us through the storms to times of calm. The deeper our convictions, the easier it is to weather the storms. God works with us in our relationship with him to deepen our convictions so we can be as solid as a rock. God was willing to work with Amos until Amos was where he needed to be. God is willing to work with us today to help us grow and mature until we become the person that he wants us to be.

V. **Vision Five: Strike the Altar.** October. Amos 9:1-2.

> *I saw the Lord standing by the altar, and he said:*

> *Strike the tops of the pillars*
> *   so that the thresholds shake.*
> *Cut off the heads of*
> *   all the people;*
> *those who are left I will kill with*
> *   the sword.*
> *Not one will get away,*
> *   none will escape.*
> *Though they dig down to the depths*
> *   of the grave,*
> *from there my hand will take*
> *   them.*
> *Though they climb up to the*
> *   heavens,*
> *from there I will bring them*
> *   down (NIV).*

The month is now October. It is time for the harvest festival in Israel. The sanctuaries at Bethel and Gilgal are prepared for sacrifices of thanksgiving to God for providing the harvest. The altars are ready and waiting. Everyone eagerly anticipates the celebration.

God now tells Amos that it is time for action. He has deepened his convictions, and now it is time for those convictions to be demonstrated. God tells Amos to "Strike the altar! Make it shake!" Amos is to strike the altar of God. This action would symbolize the way God was about to strike Israel. And yet it was more than a symbolic gesture. This was literally the beginning of

God's judgment. Amos was to lift his hand and with hammer or staff strike the pillars of the altar with such force that the entire foundation of the altar would be shaken. He was to topple the pillars upon the heads of the priests and other dignitaries who would certainly attempt to stop him. This was no small symbolic gesture. God prompted Amos to attack the sacrificial altar at Bethel and begin his judgment upon Israel.

This story reminds us of Jesus' visit to the temple of Jerusalem in John 2. Jesus and Amos were faced with the same dilemma. How could one person make a difference when the situation had gotten so sour? Should I take a stand against the selected authorities of the day? Will this one act really make a difference? For both of these prophets their relationship with the Father led them to be prophets of action. They could have sat idly by like everyone else. Instead they took a stand. They took action and initiated a change.

We must be ready to "Strike the altar!" in our lives as well. If we are struggling with impurity, strike the altar and pray unceasingly for purity. When we are consistently inconsistent, strike the altar and beg God for the conviction to change. If we are doubtful, afraid or hesitant, then strike the altar and change. If our evangelism gets stale, strike the altar and share with people. The toughest part of change is taking the first step. Fear and doubt paralyze us. "Strike the Altar!" Often action will dispel the fear.

In six months time, from April to October, God took Amos from being an emotional and sentimental seer to becoming a powerful *nabi*. The journey was not an easy one. Amos had to face his sentimentality and emotionalism. He had to see that his sentimentality was hurting God's people. When Amos grew rebellious, God continued to work with him until he learned to accept God's terms. God then deepened Amos' convictions knowing that the time of action was right around the corner. And when God asked Amos to act, he requested no less than that Amos strike the sacrificial altar at Bethel, one of the most sacred symbols in all of Israel. Six months earlier Amos was not ready for the task. But God prepared him. He turned him into a prophet.

God is willing to work with us to help us realize our full potential as disciples. For us, his tutoring might take six months or six years. The time isn't important; God is going for our hearts and he is willing to wait. The first step is acceptance. We must accept that God desires all of our talent, all of our heart, all of our drive to be used for him. Once we get past the emotions and the rebellion, God's task is much more simple. He will deepen our convictions and get us to the point where we are ready for action. What will he ask of us? For each person his request will be different. The important thing is not what he will ask; but when he asks, will we be ready. The message of Amos is: Get ready, because God will ask.

The Hymn of Amos

In May, God spoke and showed me his way. It didn't seem right. Something was wrong. I thought of old friends, my family, and my teachers. Frozen by sentimentality, I watched the days roll by like water in a flowing brook.

In July, God spoke again and showed me his way more clearly. I knew he was right. My gut told me so, but I stiffened my jaw and rebelled. In the heat of summer, I was as cold as ice.

In August, God broke through my wall. He convinced me that his way was right. He had been right all along, but my sentimentality and my rebellious heart blinded me to his truth.

During September, God worked on my convictions. He wanted me to see as he saw and to think as he thought. There was no room for doubt, fear or hesitation. God wanted all of my heart.

Then October, from conviction to action. The altar stood as an icon for the deity of laziness, impurity, pride and avarice. I picked up the hammer of God and with all my might I struck a blow that shattered the altar and freed my soul.

The months have passed and now I have become the prophet of God.

—G. Steve Kinnard, October 1991.

References

Anderson, F. and D. Freedman. *Amos*. Anchor Bible. 1989.

Cripps, Richard S. *A Critical and Exegetical Commentary on the Book of Amos*. 1929.

Edgehill, E. A. *The Book of Amos*. 1914.

Honeycutt, Roy Lee. *Amos and His Message*. 1963.

Jeremias, J. *Amos*. Old Testament Library. 1998.

Kapelrud, A. S. *Central Ideas in Amos*. 1961.

Marsh, J. *Amos and Micah*. 1959.

Mays, J. *Amos*. Old Testament Library. 1969.

McFadyen, J. E. *A Cry for Justice*. 1912.

McKeating, H. *Amos, Hosea, Micah*. 1971.

Mitchell, H. G. *Amos, an Essay in Exegesis*. 1900.

Neher, A. *Amos*. 1950.

Paul, S. *Amos*. Hermeneia. 1991.

Smith, G. *Amos*. Christian Focus. 1998.

_____. *Hosea, Amos, Micah*. The NIV Application Commentary. 2001.

Von Orelli, C. *The Twelve Minor Prophets*. 1893.

Watts, John D. W. *Vision and Prophecy in Amos*. 1958.

Wolff, H. W. *Joel and Amos*. 1977.

Jonah Ben Amittai
The Prophet of God's
Universal Love

It is clear that in the main the story of Jonah is an attempt to sketch the mission of Israel and to some extent the spirit in which she set about her task. Thus Nineveh is the heathen world, and Jonah the prophet is the nation of Israel. It is hers to tell the world the will of her God, and to call men to repentance. But in the very attempt to fulfill her task—and the attempt is only made reluctantly—she shows a spirit of narrow vindictiveness, and has to be taught that the universal God who has chosen her for a special purpose cares also for the other sheep who are not of that fold.[28]
- Theodore H. Robinson, OT scholar

The person Jonah is one of the best-remembered biblical characters. People otherwise largely ignorant of the Scriptures' content have heard about Jonah and the "whale." In this impression two significant issues are rather accurately hinted at: (1) the person of Jonah and his personal experience are central to the message of the book that bears his name, as contrasted to, for example Samuel or Amos; (2) the book is written about Jonah biographically rather than reflecting primarily the message he preached, as contrasted to all other Old Testament prophetic books.[29]
—Douglas Stuart, OT professor

1. Date

Jonah prophesied during the reign of Jeroboam II the son of Joash (II Kings 14:25). Thus, we can give him dates around 780-740 BC or perhaps slightly earlier. He was a contemporary of both Amos and Hosea. Liberal scholars date the book around 430 BC. They see Jonah as an apocryphal story that was circulated in the fifth century BC to counter the nationalistic tone of Israel during the time of Ezra and Nehemiah.

2. Location: Nineveh, the capital of Assyria.

3. Purpose

Though Jonah was a prophet of Israel, his message was directed to Nineveh, the capital of Assyria. The bigoted prophet declared a message of doom and destruction to the people of Nineveh (Jonah 3:4). The book portrays the universality of God's love, even for the heathen nations. The book contains an eight-word message, "Yet in 40 days Nineveh shall be destroyed."

4. Theme

With great skill, the book of Jonah in four short chapters calls Israel to repentance and reminds her of her mission—to preach to all the nations the breadth, length and depth of God's mercy and forgiveness (Gen. 12:1-3; Is. 42:6-7, 49:6).

5. Meaning of Name

This book derives its name from the main character *Yonah* (Hebrew) or *Ionas* (Greek), which means "dove" or "pigeon."

6. Audience: Directly—Nineveh, the capital of Assyria. Indirectly—the nation of Israel.

7a. Short Outline:

I. Jonah's Disobedience—Running Away From God, 1:1-17.

A. God's command to preach to Nineveh and
Jonah's flight to Tarshish, 1:1-3.
  B. God's miracles, 1:4-17.
    1. The storm, 1:4-14.
    2. The calm, 1:15.
    3. The great fish, 1:17.

II. Jonah's Prayer—Running to God, 2:1-9.

III. Jonah's Preaching at Nineveh—Running With God,
3:1-10.
  A. Message proclaimed, 3:1-4
  B. Nineveh repents, 3:5-9.
  C. God spares the city, 3:10.

IV. Jonah's Complaint—Running Ahead of God, 4:1-11.
  A. Jonah's anger at God's mercy and love, 4:1-5.
  B. The Lesson of the Plant, 4:6-11.

7b. Extended Outline:

1:1-16—Jonah's call to preach.
1:1-2—Jonah's call.
1:3—Jonah's rebellion. He flees to Tarshish, a southern point in Spain representing the farthest point Jonah could sail away from Nineveh.
1:4-6—God causes a great wind to threaten the safety of the ship.
1:7—The sailors cast lots, and the lot falls upon Jonah.
1:8-10—Jonah confesses the greatness of God to the sailors.
1:11-15—The men decide to throw Jonah overboard.
1:16—The sailors sacrifice and make vows to Yahweh. Jonah becomes a missionary of Yahweh in spite of himself.

1:17-2:10—Jonah is miraculously saved.

1:17—God prepares a great fish, which swallows Jonah.

2:1-9—Jonah's prayer. Jonah composes a song of thanksgiving while he is in the belly of the great fish.

2:10—Jonah is delivered upon dry land.

3:1-10—Jonah obeys the second call to preach to Nineveh.

3:1-4—Jonah receives his new call and preaches in Nineveh.

3:5—The people respond to Jonah's message by repenting. They fast and wear sackcloth as a sign of their repentance.

3:6-9—The king repents and calls for a national fast for repentance.

3:10—God forgives Nineveh.

4:1-11—Jonah protests against God's mercy.

4:1-2—Jonah lashes out against God's treatment of Nineveh.

4:3-5—Jonah despairs to the point of wishing to die. He exits the city to be in solitude.

4:6—God once again finds Jonah and this time causes a plant to grow and provide him with shade.

4:7-8—God causes a worm to destroy the plant and then sends an east wind to afflict Jonah. Jonah again desires to die.

4:9-10—God uses the plant to teach Jonah a lesson. If Jonah has compassion on the plant, cannot God have compassion on Nineveh?

4:11—God shows mercy on the 120,000 innocent citizens of Nineveh. The reference to the cattle demonstrates that God cares about the lowest of animals.

8. Memory Work
  Jonah 2:8
  Those who cling to worthless
    idols
  forfeit the grace that could be theirs (NIV).

  Jonah 4:2b
  I knew that you are a gracious
    and compassionate God,
  slow to anger and abounding in love,
    a God who
  relents from sending calamity (NIV).

9. Special Notes

I. Uniqueness of Jonah:
  a. The book is the only written prophet cast in narrative form.

  b. Jonah is the only:
  (1) Minor prophet in whose career the miraculous plays a prominent role.
  (2) Minor prophet whose major activity is on foreign soil.
  (3) Old Testament character represented as taking a trip on the Mediterranean.
  (4) Minor prophet mentioned by Jesus.
  (5) Old Testament character to whom Jesus compares himself (Matthew 12:38-41, 16:4; Luke 11:29-32).

II. Miracles?
  The miracles in the book point to the fact that God is in control of the destinies of nations and of individuals. The book of Jonah is a book more about God than Jonah. John D. W. Watts, in the Cambridge commentary on Jonah, writes, "God is the dominant character from beginning to end. He is Yahweh—the Lord—to Jonah as to any Israelite. Foreigners simply call him God. The prophet is the next character."[30] The miracles demonstrate that

God cares for his people enough to interrupt the laws of nature in order to display his love. Here are some of the miracles in Jonah:

a. The storm arose at the most appropriate time and quieted when Jonah was thrown into the sea.

b. The great fish swallowed Jonah, rescuing him from the sea, and vomiting him upon dry ground. Scholars have unsuccessfully tried to identify this great fish (*dag gadol*, in the Hebrew) for years. Many follow the King James translation and think of it as a whale. Others attempt to identify it with a shark, which could have inhabited the Mediterranean. Some look for modern examples of men being swallowed by fish to prove the historicity of Jonah's story. Some refer to James Bartley who in 1891 claimed to have lived in the belly of a sperm whale for a day and a half.[31] However, the wife of the captain of Mr. Bartley's ship later categorically denied this account. These arguments are superfluous because God especially prepared this fish for this specific purpose.

c. The entire city of Nineveh was moved to repentance by Jonah's message.

d. A plant miraculously appeared to provide shade for Jonah. It later withered and died.

III. Historicity of Jonah.

Critics of the historicity of Jonah use four arguments to attack Jonah's historicity.

(1) Scholars argue that no one writing in the eighth century BC would have referred to the king of Assyria as the king of Nineveh. They believe this type of cataloging would only have occurred much later.

This argument fails to take into account that the Biblical writers at times substituted the name of the capital city for the name of the nation. Ahab could be called "the king of Samaria" as easily as "the king of Israel" (I Kings 21:1). Also, Ben-Hadad could be spoken of as "the king of Damascus" as easily as "the king of Syria" (II Chronicles 24:23).

(2) Critics note that Nineveh is spoken of in the past tense in Jonah 3:3. This is simply the author's way of stating that upon his first visit to Nineveh it was already a city of great size.

(3) Critics attack Jonah's description of the city. Jonah describes the city as being so large that it took three days to walk across it. Critics say the city was not this large, but Jonah is not referring to a walking tour of the city. The context tells us that he was walking through the city preaching God's message. The city of Nineveh contained some 600,000 citizens at the time. Jonah was not interested in seeing how quickly he could get around the city. He walked, got the attention of a crowd, and delivered Yahweh's message. This is the only way to make sense of this passage.

(4). Critics note that a heathen city the size of Nineveh would not have repented in the dramatic way that Jonah records. How could the king have possibly asked all of his citizens to clothe themselves and their animals in sackcloth? They say this event is fictitious. If this event had happened, why is it not recorded in the Assyrian annals or in another part of the Bible? Certainly it would have been nothing short of miraculous for the entire city to repent.

But is that not exactly what the book of Jonah is saying? God is the moving force in Jonah. To doubt that this event could have happened is to doubt the power of God. Jonah had no doubt that God could have accomplished this feat. He believed it so deeply that he tried to prevent it from happening by rebelling against God and sailing to Spain.

In proof of the historicity of Jonah, one may argue:
(1) Jonah was a historical character.
(2) The book presents itself as history.
(3) The testimony of Jesus implies the historicity of the Jonah narrative (Mt. 12:38-41).

IV. Interpretation:

One's view of the historicity of Jonah will determine his or her interpretation of the book. If you believe the book to be fictitious, then you interpret the book as a parable or an allegory. If you believe the book to be historical, then you glean direct lessons from the life of Jonah and from his prophetic message.

10. Historical Context

Nineveh was one of the greatest cities of the ancient world. It had a rich history in the Middle East and was already a well-established city before Jonah visited it. The city reached its zenith under the reign of Sennacherib of Assyria.

Today the ruins of Nineveh occupy two mounds in Iraq across the Tigris River from the modern city of Mosul. Quyundijiq is a mound, which runs about one mile long and 650 yards wide and 90 feet high. Alongside of Quyundijiq runs the much smaller mound Nebi Yunus. The mounds have been excavated for more than 140 years now, although the excavation of Nebi Yunus is limited because it is the foundation of a Muslim cemetery. The wall surrounding the city is still visible and it runs for seven and one-half miles. From the wall it is one and one-half miles to the center of the city.

11. The Person

The only Old Testament reference to Jonah outside of the book which bears his name is found in II Kings 14:25. Here we learn that Jonah was from the town of Gath-Hepher, which was located a few miles north of Nazareth in the Northern Kingdom of Samaria. Gath-Hepher was a city of moderate size located within the tribal boundary of Zebulun.

Jonah was a contemporary of Jeroboam II, Amos and Hosea. Jonah predicted the success of certain military campaigns of Jeroboam II. Jeroboam II wanted to regain territory from Syria that once belonged to Israel.

Jonah was a nationalist. He was pro-Israel to the core. He loathed Assyria because of its power and its incessant desire to control Israel. As we understand Jonah, we get the picture that he opposed any person or any group that was an enemy of Israel.

From his work we can deduce that Jonah was a disciplined and dedicated prophet. As chapter two of his book attests, Jonah was a poet. He had an extremely rebellious and stubborn streak. This stubbornness was vented even against God.

Jonah was called by God to go to Nineveh and preach repentance in the name of Yahweh to that city. The capital of Assyria, Nineveh, was located 500 miles east of Palestine. When Jonah fled from God, most scholars believe that he was heading for Tartessus in Spain some 2,000 miles west of Palestine. Not only was Jonah heading in the opposite direction of Nineveh, he was attempting to place 2,500 miles between himself and Nineveh. Jonah embarked from Joppa, which was 50 miles from his hometown and the only harbor on the Palestinian coast below Mount Carmel.

John D. W. Watts sums up the life of Jonah by stating:

> Jonah was a highly skilled writer versed in the literature of prophecy and the Psalms. He was conversant with the ways of sailors and of the royal courts. His experiences ranged from Joppa to Nineveh. He was a man of conviction, holding fast to the best and most universal elements in Israel's religious heritage. In this book he poses questions for his generation and ours in those, which are put to Jonah by the sailors and by God himself.[32]

12. The Call

"Go and preach to the people of Nineveh." This was the call of Jonah. As Amos was called to go into Bethel and begin judgment against Northern Israel, so Jonah was called for a specific purpose at a specific time. Jonah was already a prophet to his own people when he received his call to go to Nineveh (Jonah 4:2-3). But this new call redefined his mission. He did not want to accept this mission.

Other prophets protested against their call, but no one

rebelled against their prophetic mission quite like Jonah. He literally ran the other way. But God did not accept "No!" for an answer. He continued to work with Jonah. God demonstrated his mercy to Jonah until Jonah finally understood God's mercy for other nations.

13. Structure and Form

Jonah is unlike the other prophetic books in that it does not contain prophetic oracles, rather, it is written in a narrative style. It is different from other Biblical narratives in that the person who should be the hero of the story (Jonah) is viewed in a negative view throughout the story. Jonah teaches us a lesson by using sensational, dramatic images. The great wind and the great fish appear at just the right moment to elicit a response from Jonah and from those who would learn from his story. It would be incorrect to consider this story a parable, however. We are not dealing with fable, but with fact. The power of Jonah comes from the fact that this story happened to a real person at a real moment in human history.

14. Theology

A. God Will Go to Great Lengths to Teach Forgiveness.

The story of Jonah is not so much about the prophet Jonah, nor is it about the people of Nineveh. The main character in Jonah is God. Jonah is a passive instrument in God's drama. It is God who is the main character, the active force throughout the book.

Jonah demonstrates the great lengths to which God will go to teach us the need to forgive. Jonah has the dubious distinction of being a prophet who wished that his message would go unheeded. He so hated the Assyrians that he chose to disobey God rather than preach to his enemies. Yet God did not allow disobedience to stifle his message. He had to teach Jonah the importance of forgiveness.

God prepared a great fish to swallow Jonah. This fish was an instrument of God's discipline. Jonah was taught the sovereignty of God while he was in the belly of the great fish. He could not hide from God. No matter where he tried to flee, God was waiting for him there. Since God has divine authority over the world, does he not have the right to decide whom he will spare and whom he will destroy? If he spares Jonah in spite of his disobedience, should he not spare Nineveh when she repents?

Yet when Nineveh repented, Jonah despaired. He was so distraught that he wished to die. This reminds us of Elijah's reaction to Jezebel's threats after the victory at Mount Carmel. After Carmel, how could Elijah doubt God? After the fish, how could Jonah doubt God? They doubted because they were weak, ordinary people just like you and me. They did not understand the whole plan of God, and they believed their view of reality was superior to his.

God had an easier time forgiving Nineveh than Jonah did. Often God has an easier time forgiving others than we do. At times God has an easier time forgiving us than we have forgiving ourselves. We forget that it is the sinner and not the saved who need mercy (Matt. 12:41).

God is the God of forgiveness. He taught Jonah the value of forgiveness. Jonah took great pleasure in a bush that grew up to give him shade. When a worm killed the plant, Jonah's bitterness increased. God rebuked Jonah saying, "What right do you have to be angry?" (Jonah 4:4, 9). Jonah had no right. He cared more about a common plant than about the 120,000 innocent people of Nineveh who knew neither right nor wrong.

God's compassion is contrasted with Jonah's lack of compassion. God's forgiving nature is contrasted with Jonah's lack of forgiveness. God went to great lengths to teach Jonah the value of forgiveness. And through Jonah, he teaches us the same lesson today.

B. Israel Was to Be a Light to the Nations.

Part of Jonah's message centers on the nature of Israel as a nation. Why did God choose Israel? What plan did he have for this nation? Jonah demonstrates that Yahweh's love extends to all nations, and Israel is responsible for demonstrating that love to the world. The test case in Jonah is God's willingness to extend his love to the hated, wicked city of Nineveh (Nahum 3:5-7).

Yahweh loves Nineveh. Even though Jonah hates Nineveh and longs for its destruction, God sends Jonah to preach his message of repentance to the city. Jonah rebels against God. After three days in a fish's belly, Jonah repents and goes to Nineveh to preach. Jonah's worst nightmare was then realized: Nineveh repents and God spares the nation.

We see a huge contrast between Jonah and God. God desires for everyone to repent. Jonah did not want Nineveh to repent. God sent prophets to foreign nations to give them the opportunity to repent. God wants to reach anyone who is willing to listen. Israel had to learn that God loved the rest of the world as much as he loved Israel. Jonah was afraid to face this fact just as much of Israel was afraid to face it. Yet the truth was evident. God loved the world. Since God loved the world, Israel needed to love the world as well. The lesson continues down to our present time. Do we love everyone the way that God loves everyone?

Israel was to be a light to the rest of the world. God created Israel as a model nation. The world would know Yahweh through Israel. The conversion of the non-Israelite is envisaged in Isaiah 2:2-4, Haggai 2:6-9 and in Zechariah 8:20-23. The story of Jonah is the story of Israel trimmed down to an individual's life. As God called Jonah to reach the foreign nations, God called Israel for the same purpose. Theodore H. Robinson writes:

> In a very real sense, then the Book of Jonah is the forerunner in Judaism of Christianity. It was on that very question of the universality of the true monotheistic faith that the church ultimately broke away from its Jewish tradition. It is not the three days and three nights that made Jonah the sign, it is the universality of the Gospel, which the book implies. It is true that Israel never learned that lesson, and that failure made her story perhaps the greatest spiritual tragedy in history. She abandoned

her world-mission, but the church accepted it, and for us who have succeeded to her heritage, it is profoundly true in Christ, that there is no other name under heaven whereby men may be saved.[33]

As Israel was unwilling to accept her role, Jonah was also unwilling. But unwilling participants have never stopped God.

15. Messianic Expectations

The book of Jonah contains no Messianic predictions. The New Testament writers do allude to the book of Jonah in two ways. First, the Gospel writers compare the time Jesus spent in the grave with the time Jonah spent in the belly of the fish (Matt. 12:39ff.). Second, the New Testament writers contrast the preaching of Jesus with that done by Jonah. They spoke of Jesus as being greater than Jonah. But if Nineveh repented at Jonah's preaching, how much more should the audience of Jesus repent (Matt. 12:41). Jesus and his disciples were familiar with the work of Jonah. They speak of Jonah as a living, breathing person who really lived in history.

16. A Lesson from Jonah

Instead of doing an exegetical treatment of one specific passage in Jonah, let's look at the book of Jonah as a whole. After all, the book is a narrative of Jonah's relationship with God; therefore, we need to understand the whole story. We will now look at Jonah chapter by chapter. Please read the Biblical text and then read my comments.

Chapter One. Running Away From God

The book of Jonah begins with a call to Jonah to go preach to the city of Nineveh. Jonah is to "cry in the ear" of the city of Nineveh. This is an interesting phrase in that it demonstrates the personal aspect of preaching.

Instead of going to Nineveh, Jonah rebelled against God and headed the other direction toward Tarshish. Nineveh was located 500 miles east of Israel. Tarshish is believed to have been in Southern Spain some 2,000 miles west of Israel. Jonah was heading the opposite direction from Nineveh. Other prophets protested their call (Isaiah and Jeremiah), but Jonah was the first to rebel against his call. He thought his plan was better than God's. We usually do not think of the prophets as being rebellious, but they were ordinary men and women just like us.

As Jonah set sail for Tarshish, God threw a great wind over the sea that threatened the safety of the ship. Remember the book of Jonah is not primarily about Jonah, but about God. God is behind all the events in the book. He is the prime mover. Despite Jonah's rebellion, God does not give up on him. He continues to work with him, forcing him to accept his plan. God provides the great wind, the great fish, the shade tree and the worm to allow Jonah to understand his mercy. God is long-suffering and patient. Though many people would have given up on Jonah, God did not. Jonah could not escape God's disturbing presence.

As the storm raged, Jonah slept in the boat. The ship's captain "cried in the ear" of Jonah. These are the same words God used to commission Jonah. Jonah was to "cry in the ear" of the people of Nineveh. Instead a pagan ship captain is crying in his ear to awaken him to God's presence. The ship's captain is now the prophet and Jonah is the stubborn, rebellious sinner in need of a prophet. Jonah was afraid of Yahweh, but notice that he could sleep like a baby through a hurricane. Jonah was confused. Rebellion leads to confusion. He was unsure of what he should or should not fear.

By casting lots, the sailors discerned that Jonah's presence on their ship had provoked the storm. They asked Jonah about his God. Jonah answered, "I am a Hebrew and I tremble before the Lord God in heaven, creator of this sea as well as dry land" (Jonah 1:9, PB). When they inquired as to how they could pacify this God, Jonah informed them that he should be thrown off the boat. The men reacted negatively to this. They were afraid that

Jonah's God might be angrier with them for such action. When they rejected the idea and began rowing to shore, God intervened. God let them know where he stood on the matter by intensifying the hurricane. The sailors understood God's prompting and threw Jonah into the sea.

The sea stopped raging as soon as Jonah was thrown overboard, and the sailors realized that the God of the Hebrews was the true God. They gave up their idols and recognized the sovereignty of Yahweh. They offered a sacrifice and made vows to the God of Israel. Jonah was evangelistic in spite of himself. He fled from Nineveh to keep from preaching, and he succeeded in getting a whole ship of sailors to acknowledge God. This is because it is God's nature to reach people. He will use the willing servant or the unwilling servant to accomplish his will. Let's make sure that we are willing servants.

Chapter Two. Running Toward God

This chapter opens with Jonah being swallowed by a "great fish." Since the King James Version translates the word as "whale" some have insisted that it was a whale. The word refers to a "great fish." It is a fish, which God has prepared for this purpose. It is irrelevant whether any man has survived in the belly of a fish for three days and nights before. Conservative scholars say there are records of this happening and liberal scholars protest the case. Whether or not it happened, God prepared this fish, and anything is possible with God.

Jonah prayed a prayer of praise and thanksgiving while inside the fish. His lowly condition helped him to realize how much he needed God. He was no longer concerned with whether his plan was better than God's plan. He simply desired to be rescued, and he knew that only God could rescue him. Some people have to hit the lowest point before they can see God for who he is. God has to humble them, break their pride, before they can acknowledge him. This was the case with Jonah.

Jonah's prayer was magnificent. Instead of running away

from the presence of God, he now longed for the presence of God. Jonah prayed:

> *My soul was ebbing away within me*
> *but I remembered the Lord*
> *and my prayer came up to you*
>
> *Up to your holy Temple*
> *as if I were there in your presence*
>
> *Those who admire mists of illusion*
> *to hide their fears*
> *abandon the compassion of openness*
>
> *But I with a thankful voice, not fearing*
> *will make of sacrifice a thanksgiving*
> *I will pay with gladness every vow I make*
>
> *It is the Lord who delivers us alive*
> *he is the captain of our praises*
>
> *I will pay my fare gladly*
> *I am his precious cargo (PB).*

Instead of heading away from God on a ship as contraband, God was now his captain, and Jonah was precious cargo in the belly of a fish.[34]

Chapter Three: Running With God

Jonah was given a second chance to obey God. God is a God of second chances. God gave Elijah a second chance after he despaired of his life in fear of Jezebel's wrath. Jesus gave the blind man of Bethsaida a second touch of grace as Jesus healed him (Mark 8). God offers us opportunity after opportunity to learn of him and to serve him. We should be thankful that he is more patient with us than we are with others. He was more patient with Jonah than Jonah was with the Assyrians.

This time Jonah obeyed. He went to the great city of Nineveh and preached God's message. Nineveh was an enormous city so wide that it took three days to cross it. From the story we know that as Jonah walked, he preached; and the people repented. Contrast the response of the people of Nineveh toward God with Jonah's responsiveness toward God. They believed and he rebelled. They repented and he lamented.

Even the king responded. He ordered everyone to fast. He demonstrated his heart through physical discomfort. The king ordered the people to wear sackcloth (burlap) and to neither eat nor drink. Even the animals were to follow this directive. They showed their repentance through deeds. Although we shy away from acts of penitence, there is something to be said for it. Physical discomfort can lead us to see the enormity of our sins and help us initiate change. The Apostle Paul stated that he buffeted his body daily so that he might keep it under control (1 Cor. 9:27).

Chapter Four. Running Ahead of God

Jonah grew bitter at God's decision to spare Nineveh. He still felt that his plan was better than God's plan. Israel's enemies should not be spared. Jonah hated the Assyrians so intensely that he desired to keep salvation from them. When God spared them, Jonah wanted to die. This is an amazing picture of a prophet. Here is a prophet who was rebellious, hostile, prejudiced, unforgiving, hateful and indignant. He was an ordinary man who faced ordinary fears. His dark side overcame his good.

Jonah not only had problems with God's actions, but he also failed to accept the very nature of God. He understood that God was merciful; he just did not like the fact that God was merciful toward the Assyrians. After God forgave Nineveh, Jonah protested:

And he prayed to the Lord, saying:
"O Lord, wasn't this the exact word and vision
I had always delivered and known you by
*   when I was still in my own country?*
This is exactly why
*   I wanted to leave your presence*
for Tarshish, before you would call me
*   a second time*
because I knew you as a gracious God
*   compassionate, long-suffering*
*   and of great kindness*
and would repent of bitterness" (Jonah 4:2-3, PB).

Jonah wanted to create God in Jonah's image. He wanted a God who would be abundantly merciful to Israel, yet show no mercy to Assyria.

The book is not just about Jonah, but also about God. Jonah hopes throughout his story that God's character will be inconsistent. Yet, God is consistent throughout. God's consistency stands in stark contrast to Jonah's inconsistency. Through Jonah, Israel is invited to reconsider her views of God and her terrible inconsistencies.

The book of Jonah demonstrates how far God will go to help a person overcome hatred and prejudice. It shows the lengths to which God will go to help someone understand his nature. God provided Jonah with a great storm, a great fish and a great repentance to show his mercy. God demonstrated to Jonah the length, breadth, depth and width of his love.

Jonah would not feel compassion for Nineveh, but he felt compassion for a plant. When God destroyed the plant that had given Jonah shade, Jonah lashed out against God. Again Jonah wanted to die. How could God have attacked this harmless plant? Why would God not allow this one pleasant thing in Jonah's life?

God compares Jonah's feeling for the plant with his own

feelings for the city of Nineveh. If Jonah could have compassion for a plant in which he had no investment, why could God not spare Nineveh?

The book of Jonah ends with a question. God asked Jonah this question, but he has continued to ask the question through the centuries first to Israel then to the church. God asks:

> *And may I not feel compassion*
> *for Nineveh, the great city*
> *which has grown up here with more than*
> *a hundred and twenty thousand men and women*
> *all of them innocent of knowing the difference*
> *between right (the hand that provides)*
> *and left—and likewise*
> *many, many animals? (Jonah 4:11, PB).*

Why was the book of Jonah written? It helps us understand the nature of God's mercy. Douglas Stuart, notes:

> Every hearer/reader may have some Jonah in him or her. All need to reflect on the questions God asks, including the final, specific, "Should I not spare Nineveh?" (4:11). Anyone who replies "Why is that such an important question?" has not understood the message. Anyone who replies "No!" has not believed it."[35]

Will God's people learn how to forgive and how to show mercy to others? Will they overcome their prejudice and accept all people the same? Will they rise above their petty hurts and accept individuals as individuals regardless of ethnic origin or social background? The ending of Jonah is still being written today. Each disciple is writing it in the practical realm of his or her daily living. How will we answer this question that God posed to Jonah?

Jonah's Tale Revisited

In pubs from Capetown to Liverpool fishermen love to tell fish stories.

The taller the mug of ale—the grander the story.

Imagine the mug, which prompted the telling of Jonah—the grandest of the grand fish stories.

But Jonah is not a story about a fish.

It is about the creator of fish, the Master Fisherman—God himself.

Jonah was not alone in the belly of the fish. He went there to escape God's presence. Instead he found God. God fought the stench of decaying fish, foul seaweed, and murky salt water for three full days and three full nights to track down, capture and win back an errant prophet.

God, the Sovereign God, creator of heaven and earth lived for three full days and three full nights tossed to and fro in the belly of a fish.

This was an incredible act of love. Yet it pales when compared to God's descent into the cold, dark, damp crust of the earth 700 years later.

God, the Sovereign God, creator of heaven and earth set up camp for three full days and three full nights in the belly of the earth. The pitch black, intolerably cold, silent earth.

This time he came to track down, capture and win back an errant humanity.

The giver of life in the place of the dead.

The builder of community alone in a tomb.

The maker of light in a place of darkness.

All in all, the stench of seaweed and decaying fish must have seemed pleasant compared to the aftermath of the cross.

Watching the seconds trickle by.

Waiting out the hours.

For three full days and three full nights in the cold, dark, damp crust of the earth.

—G. Steve Kinnard, Feb. 1992.

References

Alders, G. C. *The Problem of the Book of Jonah.* 1948.

Allen, L. C. *The Books of Joel, Obadiah, Jonah, and Micah.* The New International Commentary on the Old Testament. 1976.

Banks, W. L. *Jonah: The Reluctant Prophet.* Everyman's Bible Commentary Series, 1966.

Fretheim, T. E. *The Message of Jonah: A Theological Commentary.* 1977.

Knight, George, A. F. *Ruth and Jonah.* 1966.

Limburg, J. *Jonah.* Old Testament Library. 1993.

McGarvey, J. W. *Jesus and Jonah.* 1952.

Myers, J. M. *The Book of Jonah.* 1959.

Nixon, R. *The Message of Jonah.* The Bible Speaks Today. 2003.

Perowne, T. T. *Obadiah and Jonah.* 1883.

Sasson, J. *Jonah.* The Anchor Bible. 1990.

Smith, B. K. *Hosea, Joel, Amos, Obadiah, Jonah.* Layman's Bible Book Commentary. 1982.

Stuart, D. *Jonah.* Word Bible Commentary. 1987.

Wade, G. W. *The Books of the Prophets Micah, Obadiah, Joel and Jonah.* Westminster Commentaries, 1925.

Watts, John D. W. *The Books of Joel, Obadiah, Jonah, Nahum, Habakkuk, and Zephaniah.* The Cambridge Bible Commentary on the New English Bible. 1975.

Woolf, H. *Jonah.* Continental. 1986.

5

Hosea Ben Beeri
The Prophet of
Unconditional Love

"My people are destroyed from a lack of knowledge."
—Hosea 4:6

Hosea was a man possessed and dominated by his love. It went to the very roots of his being, and so fully did it absorb him that no sin or folly on Gomer's part could shake it. It was no mere explosive flash of strong emotion that had kindled in his life, it was a consuming fire shut up in his bones, which no rejection could weaken and no suffering quench. In all the world's literature there is no record of human love like his.[36]
—*Theodore H. Robinson, OT scholar*

1. Date

Hosea prophesied during the reigns of Uzziah (783-742), Jotham (750-735), Ahaz (735-715) and Hezekiah (715-687), kings of Judah (Hosea 1:1). He began his ministry while Jeroboam II occupied the throne in Samaria. Thus his work took place during the period of 783-687 BC, more concisely around 750-715 BC. Hosea was a contemporary of Micah and Isaiah.

2. Location: The Northern Kingdom of Israel.

3. Purpose

Hosea urged the nation of Israel to acknowledge its sinful condition and repent. Israel is pictured as a wife guilty of adultery, but God is like the loving and faithful husband. Hosea's family is used in an allegorical manner to portray the message of Yahweh. The relationship between Hosea and Gomer represents the relationship between Yahweh and Israel. The book graphically illustrates Israel's rejection of Yahweh and points her toward repentance.

4. Theme

Hosea has been called "the prophet of love." He might more appropriately be called "the prophet of unconditional love." Through his own experience with unfaithful Gomer, he came to know the heartbreak that was God's heartbreak. Hosea identified idolatry as spiritual adultery. In spite of Israel's spiritual prostitution, God still loved Israel with an unconditional love.

5. Meaning of Name

The Hebrew term is *Hoshea*, which means "salvation." The Greek and Latin use the name *Osee*.

6. Audience

Unlike Amos who was a Southerner, Hosea was a member of the Northern Kingdom of Israel and thus prophesied to his own people.

7. Outline

I. Hosea's personal story. His marriage experience is a symbol of God's experience with Israel, Hosea 1-3.

II. Israel's moral, spiritual and political unfaithfulness, Hosea 4-13.
  A. Denunciation of pride, idolatry and corruption, Hosea 4-8.

B. The certainty of the approaching punishment of the Northern Kingdom, Hosea 9-10.

C. A parenthetical utterance dealing with the triumph of divine love and mercy, Hosea 11:1-11.

D. Destruction as the result of Israel's infidelity and rebellion, Hosea 11:12-13:16.

III. Israel's conversion and God's promise of renewal, Hosea 14.

7b. Extended Outline

1-3 Hosea's Marriage

1:1—The Introduction
1:2-9—Hosea's biographical narrative
1:2—Hosea was commanded to marry a prostitute.
1:3-5—Hosea married Gomer and she gave birth to Jezreel.
1:6-7—Gomer conceived a daughter and named her "Unloved."
1:8-9—Gomer conceived a son and named him "No People of Mine."
1:10-2:1—A glimpse of the future of Israel
2:2-23—The story of Hosea paralleled to the history of Yahweh and his unfaithful wife, Israel.
3:1-5—Hosea took back Gomer in spite of her infidelity.

4-13—Israel's unfaithfulness and God's faithfulness.
4:1-3—The corruption of Israel
4:4-11—Condemnation of the priests
4:12-14—Condemnation of the worship in Israel
4:15—Judah is warned of her sin.
4:16-19—Israel is compared to a stubborn heifer.

5:1-7—The condemnation of the rulers of Israel
5:8-12—The Syro-Ephraimite war of 735-734 BC
5:13-14—The folly of trusting in foreign allies
5:15—Yahweh will turn his back on Israel.

6:1-6—Israel's worldly sorrow
6:7-7:2—The sins of Israel

7:3-7—Israel's politics are full of conspiracy and intrigue.
7:8-12—Israel cannot trust in foreign power.
7:13-16—Israel's ingratitude

8:1-3—The watchman sounds the warning.
8:4-7—Anarchy and idolatry in Israel
8:8-10—Israel cannot trust in foreign powers.
8:11-13—Formal worship is lacking in power.
8:14—Teaching against the extravagance in building

9:1-6—The pain of exile
9:7-9—The persona of a prophet
9:10-14—Israel's punishment for her crimes at Baal-peor
9:15-17—Israel's punishment for her crimes at Gilgal

10:1-8—The destruction of Israel's cultic objects
10:9-10—Prophecy against Gibeah
10:11-12—A chance for Israel to repent
10:13-15—Israel's end is foretold.

11:1-6—The vengeance of God
11:7-9—God's love is greater than his vengeance.
11:10-12—Israel's return from exile

12:1-2—Pronouncement against Israel's religion
12:3-6—Pronouncement against Jacob
12:7-8—Israel's greed

12:9-10—Possible reconciliation between Israel and Yahweh
12:11-12—The sins of Israel
12:13-14—Pronouncement against Jacob and Ephraim

13:1-3—Teaching against idolatry
13:4-8—Punishment for ingratitude
13:9-11—The end of the monarchy
13:12-16—Israel's doom is certain.

14:1-9—The conversion of Israel
14:10—Postscript.

8. Memory Work

Hosea 2:19-20
I will betroth you to me forever;
I will betroth you in
righteousness and justice,
in love and compassion.
I will betroth you in faithfulness,
and you will acknowledge the
Lord (NIV).

Hosea 4:6
My people are destroyed from lack of knowledge (NIV).

Hosea 6:6
For I desire mercy, not sacrifice,
and acknowledgment of God
rather than burnt
offerings (NIV).

Hosea 8:7
They sow the wind
and reap the whirlwind (NIV).

Hosea 10:12
Sow for yourselves righteousness,
reap the fruit of unfailing love,
and break up your unplowed
ground;
for it is time to seek the Lord,
until he comes
and showers righteousness on
you (NIV).

Hosea 12:6
But you must return to your God;
maintain love and justice,
and wait for your God always.

Hosea 13:14
I will ransom them from the power
of the grave;
I will redeem them from death.
Where, O death, are your plagues?
Where, O grave, is your
destruction?

Hosea 14:9
Who is wise? He will realize these
things.
Who is discerning? He will
understand them.
The ways of the Lord are right;
the righteous walk in them,
but the rebellious stumble in
them.

9. Special Notes

A. Interpretation: Hosea's marital experience has been interpreted three ways:

(1). The literal view: Gomer was a prostitute when Hosea married her.

(2). The modified literal view: Although not a prostitute when Hosea married her, Gomer had propensities in that direction.

(3). The symbolic view: No literal marriage is involved; the account concerning Gomer is a parable.

B. Children: Observe the symbolic names of Hosea's children.

(1). *Jezreel*—double meaning, "God scatters" and "God sows." This name is taken from the place where Jehu executed his bloody purge upon Israel (II Kings 9).

(2). *Lo'ruhamah*—"not pitied"

(3). *Lo'ammi*—"not my people"

The names of the children illustrate that Yahweh has rejected Israel because she rejected him.

In chapter two, Yahweh uses a word play with these names to illustrate that he will one day accept his people back.

C. Unlike other prophets who clearly present themselves as a messenger sent from God, Hosea lives the message experiencing it through the pain and anguish of his relationship with Gomer. Hosea is on a quest. His quest is to salvage Israel's identity, which has been contaminated by the foreign religions surrounding her. The decline began when Zechariah succeeded the throne of Jeroboam in 746 BC. E. W. Heaton, author of *The Old Testament Prophets*, writes:

> Like a good actor, Hosea does not merely mouth his lines; he lives his part. And since his part as prophet was created by a knowledge of God so authenticating as to remove all doubt and ambiguity, he was free to be himself and say what he thought.[37]

D. Hosea has the distinction of being the only independent prophet from the Northern Kingdom who ministered to his own people. One fact that substantiates Hosea being from the north is his frequent use of Ephraim to signify the Northern Kingdom of Israel. Ephraim was the more personal name of Israel preferred by its citizens.

E. The Hebrew text of Hosea is probably the most corrupt of all of the books of the Old Testament. This problem might have occurred because Hosea penned his work just before the Northern Kingdom was defeated and was carried into exile. The book of Hosea could have been taken to Judah and thus survived through the centuries.

F. Hosea has greatly influenced both the Hebrew prophets who followed him, as well as the writers of the New Testament. John F. A. Sawyer, author of an excellent introduction to the Old Testament Minor Prophets, writes:

> The book of Hosea is the longest of the twelve prophets and in it more than anywhere else, in spite of many textual and exegetical problems, we can hear the original voice of eighth-century prophecy speaking out boldly against materialism and social injustice. Here appear for the first time a spiritual dimension and an ethical idealism, which were to have a profound influence on later tradition, including Paul and early Christianity. Maybe Hosea's was the first in the long sequence of radical voices of Biblical prophecy.[38]

10. Historical Context

After Amos, the situation in the Northern Kingdom grew progressively worse. Hosea's ministry parallels this time of decay. Hosea began his work around 750 BC, during the final years of Jeroboam II (786-746). Jeroboam II was the last of the strong leaders of Israel. After him, six kings succeeded to the throne during a twenty-five year span, but only one of these (Menahem) transmitted the kingship to his son. These events are recorded in II Kings 15-17. The theme of this period is conspiracy and murder. Theodore H. Robinson notes:

> The reign of Zechariah, Jeroboam's son, is given as six months; that of his murderer, Shallum, as one month; that of Pekahiah, son of Menahem, as two years. All were assassinated by their successors, as was also eventually Pekah, the murderer of Pekahiah.[39]

This notorious time in Israel's history was the beginning of the end. The decline began when Zechariah succeeded the throne of Jeroboam in 746. Zechariah reigned only six months before Shallum, a rival army officer, assassinated him. Shallum was murdered within a month by Menahem (745-738), who was an extremely ruthless leader. II Kings 15:16 notes that Menahem attacked his own city of Tappuah, killing the inhabitants, even ripping open the wombs of the women who were with child.

By this time, the influence of foreign powers was felt in the area around Israel. Assyria was the dominant force. The great days when Ahab of Israel and Ben-Hadad of Syria checked the tide of Assyrian domination at the battle of Qarqar was long past. The Assyrian aggression was renewed with the accession of Tiglath-Pileser III in 745 BC. This king was aggressive and ambitious, desiring to conquer lands and take enemies captive. Although Amos never named the specific threat to Israel's security, Hosea specifically mentioned that it was Assyria (7:11, 11:5, 14:3).

Menahem along with other kings from the land of Palestine were able to hold off Assyria by offering tribute. The Assyrians required a large amount of tribute, which Menahem raised by taking money from the merchants who had grown rich under the reign of Jeroboam II.

In 738, Menahem's crown was passed to his son Pekahiah. Pekahiah did not wear the crown very long because Pekah (737-732), with the help of fifty soldiers, successfully gained control of the kingdom in a *coup d'etat*. In 734, Pekah joined forces with Rezin, the King of Damascus, and invaded Judah to attack King Ahaz. This attack was prompted because Ahaz would not join Pekah and Rezin in a coalition to attack Tiglath-Pileser of Assyria. This battle between Judah against the combined forces of Israel and Syria is known as the Syro-Ephraimitic War (II Kings 16:5-9). Ahaz made a brilliant move strategically by appealing to Tiglath-Pileser for help to subdue the aggressors. Assyria responded aggressively and quickly squashed the army of Pekah and Rezin. In 735, Tiglath-Pileser took Gilead and deported the people of Naphtali to Assyria. This was the beginning of the dismemberment of the Northern Kingdom. After his failure, Pekah was murdered and replaced by Hoshea (732-724) who was nothing more than a puppet of the Assyrian government.

When Tiglath-Pileser died in 727, Hoshea saw this as his chance to break away from Assyrian domination. He attempted to form an alliance with So, the king of Egypt, against the Assyrian forces. Hoshea did not count on the fortitude of Tiglath-Pileser's successor, Shalmaneser V. Hoshea was arrested by Shalmaneser V and the capital city Samaria was placed under siege for three years until it fell in 722/721 BC. Before Samaria fell, Shalmaneser V died and was succeeded by his son Sargon II (722-705). Sargon claimed to have deported 27,290 people to Assyria. After Samaria fell, he then replaced those he took into exile with foreigners from nearby countries. Israel fell at the hands of the Assyrian aggressor just as Amos and Hosea had predicted.

Hosea's ministry spanned these turbulent years in Israel. He witnessed both the stability of the years under Jeroboam II and the instability of the many rulers that followed. Through it all he knew the future of Israel was not in the hands of kings and captains but in the hands of Yahweh, who had called Israel into existence centuries earlier.

11. The Person

Almost nothing is really known of Hosea apart from a few

scattered references in the book of Hosea. His ministry took place during the reigns of the Judean kings Uzziah, Jotham, Ahaz and Hezekiah. He also prophesied during the reign of the Israelite king Jeroboam II and the six kings who followed him. He was a contemporary of Isaiah (1:1; cf. Is. 1:1), and was witness with him of the collapse of the affluence and might of Israel into the hands of the Assyrians in 734-721 BC. Like Amos before him, he faced rejection because of his call (9:7-8).

The information we have about Hosea centers on his unhappy marriage and dismal family life. This information comes from two small collections. Chapter one, the first account, tells the story in the third person, just as much of Jeremiah's life is told by one of his friends. The other, briefer, and more poignant narrative, chapter three, is in the prophet's own words.

What information do we have? We know that Hosea was the son of an otherwise unknown and unidentifiable Beeri (1:1). Hosea was from Israel and his ministry was probably located in Samaria, the capital city, around the sanctuaries of Bethel and Gilgal. Hosea married a cult prostitute named Gomer, and together they had three children. It is uncertain whether or not the children were legitimately Hosea's; nevertheless, he accepted them and reared them as his own.

Hosea was different from Amos in that Amos was from the country and Hosea was a city man. His analogies and examples are drawn from town life. Since his most striking figure of speech was borrowed from the bakeshop (7:6-8), Theodore H. Robinson suggests that Hosea might possibly have been a baker by trade.[40]

Whatever his trade, he had a rich sense of how God acted in history with Israel. He based his prophecy on the basic tenets of Israel's faith—the election of the patriarchs, the liberation of the Hebrews from Egyptian domination, the guiding hand of God through the wilderness experience and the gift of the fertile land to Israel.

12. The Call

Hosea offers an interesting perspective on the meaning of

nabi (prophet). Hosea 9:7-8 reads:

> *The days of punishment are*
> *coming,*
> *the days of reckoning are at*
> *hand.*
> *Let Israel know this:*
> *Because your sins are so many*
> *and your hostility so great*
> *the prophet (nabi) is considered a fool,*
> *the inspired man a maniac.*
> *The prophet (nabi), along with my God,*
> *is the watchman over Ephraim,*
> *yet snares await him on all his*
> *paths, and hostility in the house of his*
> *God (NIV).*[41]

When we understand the price Hosea paid to be a prophet, these words become clear. Hosea was called not just to be a prophet, but for his entire life to be an example to the nation of Israel and to all of humanity. Nearly all of what we know of Hosea relates solely to his unhappy experience of love and his marriage to the prostitute Gomer.

God called Hosea not just to be his spokesman, but also to speak in a particular and peculiar way. Hosea 1:2-3 says:

When the Lord began to speak through Hosea, the Lord said to him, "Go, take to yourself an adulterous wife and children of unfaithfulness, because the land is guilty of the vilest adultery in departing from the Lord." So he married Gomer daughter of Diblaim, and she conceived and bore him a son.

This was the call of Hosea. It was the most radical call any prophet received with the exception of Jesus. God's call to Hosea affected not only his and his wife's life, but that of his children as well. They had to live with Hosea's stigma. Even their names signify they were bastards, stigmatized by Hosea's call.

Hosea's call was so radical that most scholars today understand it as figurative and not literal. They question how God could ask anyone to marry a prostitute. Yet we must remember that in the Old Testament, the society was greater than the individual. Klaus Koch, author of *The Prophets: Volume One—The Assyrian Period*, has expounded on this concept of the corporate personality of Israel by writing:

> But ancient Israel did not as yet pursue the respectable paths of middle-class morality. Rather, it reckoned with the fact that God himself can disregard individual human happiness for the sake of the common good. Nothing in the story (of Hosea) permits us to doubt that it was sheer fact. So for months and years Hosea experienced his family misery as a symbolic happening, pregnant with significance, which ran its course for the sake of the people. He did not permit himself to consider his personal happiness. Having been appointed Yahweh's messenger—destined, indeed, for a gesture anticipating future history—he no longer had a private life of his own.[42]

This idea of corporate personality, where the individual views the needs of the society as greater than his own, is expressed throughout the Old Testament. But nowhere in the Old Testament is corporate personality expressed more radically than in the call of Hosea.

The extravagant ways that other prophets chose to get their message across to people also should not be forgotten. Isaiah is mentioned as walking around naked for three years to illustrate how Assyria would take Israel into captivity. Jeremiah was thrown into a cistern and left for dead because he would not kowtow to the king. God told Ezekiel that his wife would die, but Ezekiel was not to shed a tear or issue one cry of grief. But Jesus of Nazareth was the most radical of all the prophets. He stretched his arms across a cross and died for the sins of humanity. If Jesus was willing to go to such an extreme to communicate the message of God's love, then Hosea's actions shouldn't surprise us at all.

13. Structure and Form

The book of Hosea is easily divided into three broad sections. The first (chapters 1-3) concerns God's love for Israel as seen in Hosea's unconditional love for his wife. The second (4:1-9) contains a long series of striking prophecies of hypocrisy, judgment, idolatry, corrupt priests and social injustice in the land. The third section of the book contains attacks on Israel and Judah and references to the early traditions of Israel's history.

Hosea mastered the use of poetic language to deliver the oracles of God. He often used this form to relate to daily matters in the lives of individuals. He excelled in the use of simile and metaphor to gain the attention of his listeners. James D. Newsome, Jr., author of *The Hebrew Prophets*, lists the expressions used by Hosea to contrast Yahweh and Israel as follows:[43]

Yahweh is like:
    A husband (2:2)
    A father (11:1)
    A physician (7:1)
    A fowler (7:12)
    A lion (5:14)
    A leopard (13:7)
    A she-bear (13:8)
    The dew (14:5
    The dawn (6:3)
    The rain (6:3)
    A cypress (14:8)
    A moth (5:12)
    Dry rot (5:12)

Israel is like:
    A wife (2:2)
    A sick person (5:13)

A silly dove (7:11)
A trained heifer (10:11)
A luxuriant grapevine (10:1)
Grapes (9:10)
The early fig (9:10)
A lily (14:5)
An olive tree (14:6)
A woman in labor (13:13)
An unborn son (13:13)
An oven (7:4)
A cake of bread (7:8)
A bow (7:16)
The morning mist and dew (13:3)
Chaff blown from the threshing floor (13:3)
Smoke that rises from the window (13:3)

This list illustrates Hosea's use of language to express God's message. Even though he might have been a farmer or a baker, he wrote beautiful, descriptive poetry that has survived for centuries.

14. Theology
I. Ephraim is unfaithful to Yahweh.

Hosea understood that Israel had placed herself in a precarious situation. She had left her lover, broken covenant with her God. Hosea spoke of this covenant relationship more profusely than any other prophet. B. W. Anderson, author of *Understanding the Old Testament*, writes:

No prophet was more profoundly aware of the Mosaic past than was Hosea. The memory of the Exodus, the sojourn in the wilderness, the covenant at Horeb, and the occupation of Canaan were always in his mind as he interpreted the events and condition of his time. In fact, he understood himself to be a successor of Moses, the great interpreter and mediator of the covenant.[44]

Since she broke covenant with God, Israel would pay for her infidelity. Ephraim was guilty of adultery, deceit and rebellion. She was disloyal and dishonest. Injustice pervaded both the domestic and international arenas. No one was willing to stop the avalanche of corruption that was destroying the nation. The sins were grievous and many. George L. Robinson[45] mentions seven reasons for Israel's national collapse in his book, *The Twelve Minor Prophets*. Consider the following:

(a.) Knowledge of God. What does God desire of humanity? Acknowledgment. God simply wants us to acknowledge him (2:14). With Hosea, to know God is no mere intellectual matter. Knowledge is an intimate relationship that comes from living with and for him. We must persistently pursue God (6:3). Without knowledge, killing, stealing and lying rule (4:1-2). Hosea testifies that people are destroyed for lack of knowledge (4:6; 13:4; John 17:3). God demands knowledge and mercy more than sacrifice (6:6). Since Israel will not acknowledge God, she will be destroyed.

(b.) Pride. When something comes easily, it is often taken for granted. Israel began to take her relationship with God for granted. She began to act as if she had chosen God instead of God choosing her. This pride led her into sin. Hosea exclaims, "Israel's arrogance testifies against them; the Israelites, even Ephraim, stumble in their sin" (5:5, *NIV*). Israel learned that "God opposes the proud, but gives grace to the humble" (I Peter 5:5, *NIV*).

(c.) Instability. Instead of consistently "walking in the way of the Lord," Israel's goodness was as a morning cloud or the dew upon the grass (6:4). She knew how to live, but she failed to meet God's standard. She continued to emphasize worship and the need for sacrifice, but the heart was missing. Once the heart is gone, worship is in vain (Mark 7:6-8).

(d.) Worldliness. Ephraim accepted the influence of her neighboring countries to the point that she forgot her loyalty to God.

This was especially disastrous in the context of worship. Images of Baal were allowed into the shrines of Yahweh. These images contaminated the Hebrew concept of God. Hosea accuses Israel by saying, "Ephraim mixes with the nation; Ephraim is a flat cake not turned over" (Hosea 7:8, NIV). Israel is half-baked. She should worship Yahweh, but she has accepted foreign influence to the point that she doesn't even know whom she worships. Israel has been corrupted from the inside out.

(e.) Corruption. If a person lives in an abnormal condition long enough, the abnormal becomes normal. This happened to Israel. Her standard became so lax that the unaccepted became the accepted. Injustice was accepted as justice. Immorality was more prevalent than morality. Lies were more common than the truth. What was sown would have to be reaped. Hosea prophesies:

> *They sow the wind*
> *and reap the whirlwind.*
> *The stalk has no head;*
> *it will produce no flour.*
> *Were it to yield grain,*
> *foreigners would swallow it up.*
> *Israel is swallowed up;*
> *now she is among the nations like a*
> *worthless thing.*
> *For they have gone up to Assyria*
> *like a wild donkey wandering alone.*
> *Ephraim has sold herself to*
> *lovers (Hosea 8:7-9, NIV).*

Israel, the jewel of God's creation, has become worthless. She is corrupt and beyond repair.

(f.) Backsliding. Hearts are easily corrupted, and once corrupted, they become hard. A heart can be so corrupted that it reaches the point of no return. When this happens there is no alternative but to start over again, begin anew. Israel had reached this point of no return. She had so deteriorated that God had no choice but to destroy what was and start afresh. God cried:

> *When Israel was a child, I*
>> *loved him,*
>> *and out of Egypt I called my son.*
> *But the more I called Israel,*
>> *the further they went from me....*
> *My people are determined to turn*
>> *from me.*
> *Even if they call to the Most High,*
>> *he will by no means exalt them*
> *(Hosea 11:1-2, 7, NIV).*

(g.) Idolatry. If God ever had a "worst nightmare" it might be this: his nation shaping stone and wood into images that they would worship. Israel accepted into her bosom the most abominable thing in God's sight—idols. Hosea 9:14-10:8 contains the list of threats and punishments charged against Israel for her idolatry. Israel had completely abandoned God, trusting in images made by hand instead of trusting in the creator who made the hand. Because of Israel's spiritual adultery, she would die.

II. Spiritual Adultery:

Hosea's relationship with Gomer established a basis for thinking of disloyalty to God as "spiritual adultery" (4:15-18, 5:4, 9:1). Israel's marriage relationship went back to a betrothal period in the wilderness of Sinai, but in Canaan she had gone after other lovers, idols. Before she could return to her husband, she must be taken back to the wilderness and reminded of her first love (2:14).

Hosea used the Hebrew root, *zena*, "to be a prostitute," with its derivative, nineteen times, always at crucial points in his narrative. Prostitution was attacked both in the literal sense (cultic prostitution) and the figurative sense (idol worshipping). The imagery merged in the cultic center of Israel. Consider Hosea 4:10-14:

They will eat but not have
enough;
they will engage in prostitution
but not increase,
because they have deserted the
Lord
to give themselves to
prostitution,
to old wine and new,
which take away the
understanding of my
people.
They consult a wooden idol
and are answered by a stick of
wood.
A spirit of prostitution leads them
astray;
they are unfaithful to their God.
They sacrifice on the mountaintops
and burn offerings on the hills,
under oak, poplar and terebinth,
where the shade is pleasant.
Therefore your daughters turn to
prostitution
and your daughters-in-law to
adultery.
I will not punish your daughters
when they turn to prostitution,
nor your daughters-in-law
when they commit adultery,
because the men themselves consort
with harlots
and sacrifice with shrine
prostitutes—
a people without understanding
will come to ruin! (NIV).

The fertility cults of Canaan negatively influenced Israel. Baal was worshipped as the god who controlled the weather, harvest and fertility. Sexual activity was at the center of Baal's worship. Israel incorporated this into her worship and prostituted herself before God.

For many of us in Western society this mixing of sexuality and worship seems a strange concept. Yet it was a normal feature of ancient, polytheistic religions, especially those based on a form of nature worship. Even today in India, certain boys are selected at birth and given to the Hindu temples to be made into eunuchs. Their testicles are tied with twine until they atrophy. The boys are then brought up to become temple prostitutes. They become the scapegoat for the wrongs of the Hindu people. I will never forget the time in Bombay when I saw a group of men dressed in saris begging in the streets. They were freed from their cages of prostitution every Tuesday and Friday to beg from the people. People feared these eunuchs because they believed they had the power to curse them. Sadly enough, they looked upon these eunuchs as holy people.

Cultic prostitution was sanctioned and sanctified in the fertility cults of Canaan. The Hebrews had a difficult time keeping this element out of the worship of Yahweh. They were not always successful. In fact, one of the Hebrew words for "harlot" is literally "holy woman."

Hosea understood that Israel had fallen into gross sin. He also was clear that indulgence in sin would delude the mind and dull the conscience. He saw the inevitable outcome of Israel's flirting with the sexual sins of the Canaanite fertility cults. He opposed the licentiousness of the Israelite festivals because they had become just like the worship of Baal. In Hosea 9:1-4, the prophet cries:

> *Do not rejoice, O Israel;*
> *do not be jubilant like the other*
> *   nations.*
> *For you have been unfaithful to*

your God;
you love the wages of a
    prostitute
    at every threshing floor.
Threshing floors and winepresses
    will not feed the people;
    the new wine will fail them.
They will not remain in the Lord's land;
Ephraim will return to Egypt
    and eat unclean food in
    Assyria.
They will not pour out wine
    offerings to the Lord,
nor will their sacrifices please
    him.
Such sacrifices will be to them like
    the bread of mourners;
all who eat them will be
    unclean.
This food will be for themselves;
    it will not come into the temple
    of the Lord (NIV).

III. Israel's religion has become corrupt.

Amos kept social injustice in the forefront of his criticism of the nation of Israel. Hosea focused on another downfall of Israel—her cult. He not only exposed the religion of the present generation as ineffective, but also brought to light the service of Baal hidden behind the service of Yahweh. Hosea branded this service as degenerate.

Hosea especially criticized the priests and religious hierarchy of Israel. They had the Torah to guide them, but they had given up on God's precepts and followed their own desires. Hosea's language is reminiscent of the Apostle Paul in 2 Timothy 4:3-4 when he speaks of the false teachers of a future time saying, "For the time will come when men will not put up with sound doctrine. Instead, to suit their own desires, they will gather around them a great number of teachers to say what their itching ears want to hear. They will turn their ears away from the truth and turn aside to myths" (NIV).

In like manner Hosea attacked the false teachers of his day. More than any other social group in the nation he chastised the priests. They were the recipients of the Torah. It was their responsibility to convey God's knowledge to the people. Yet they had failed in their responsibility. The institution of cultic worship was flourishing, but the heart was absent. The people had not forgotten their sacrifices and burnt offerings, but they had forgotten about mercy and grace. In Hosea 6:6, God declared, "For I desire goodness, not sacrifice; obedience to God, rather than burnt offerings" (Tanakh). The answer for Israel was not to give up on the institution of worship, but to be sure that the heart was placed in worship.

IV. A price must be paid for sin.

The fact that God was forgiving and his hesed flowed in an unconditional way toward Israel did not mean there was no culpability for sin. Hosea taught that the penalty for sin must correspond to the offense. Since Israel had violated God in such a crass and horrific way, her penalty would be severe: destruction and exile.

God punished Israel not because he wanted to satisfy a sadistic desire for retribution. His desire was to see Israel repent. But sin has its consequences. Often these consequences are excruciatingly painful. If heeded, they could be educational and remedial. If sin had no consequence, we would never learn from our mistakes.

Israel had to learn from her mistakes. Even though God had chosen her, freed her from slavery, made her into a nation and promised her glory; she turned her back on him. God would punish her so she would seek him out in her distress. Hosea 5:15 states:

Yes, I am going to return to my dwelling place
until they confess their guilt and seek my face;
they will search for me in their misery (JB).

V. Yahweh's love is unconditional.

Hesed: Coverdale (1533 AD) and those who came after him translated *hesed* as "loving kindness," but it is also can be translated as "mercy." It can also be thought of as unconditional love, similar to agape love in the New Testament. The term occurs five times in Hosea and is related to grace and loyalty (2:19, 4:1, 6:6, 10:12, 12:6). Hesed implies covenant loyalty, and does not occur in Amos.

Hosea believed in the *hesed* of God. He experienced it in his own life, and he saw it expressed in Israel's history.

Hosea has greatly contributed to our understanding of *hesed.* Outside of the example of the cross, there is no greater example of unconditional love than the love of Hosea for Gomer. Hosea understood the divine love of God for humanity because of his marriage. Theodore H. Robinson states:

And, being what he was, he knew from his own experience that there is no true love apart from pain. It may
almost be said that the converse is true, that there is no
pain of the deepest kind without love. The ability to endure is the test of the capacity for love, and its fuller and
richer development is to be attained only through suffering.[46]

Yahweh's *hesed* was seen in the fact that God chose Israel to be his people and not vice versa. Hosea portrayed this action by painting a sensitive vignette of Israel as God's son whom he caressed, fed and taught to walk only to see this son reject his love. Hosea 11:1-4 reads:

When Israel was a child,
I loved him

> *and out of Egypt I called my son.*
> *But the more I called Israel,*
> *the further they went from me.*
> *They sacrificed to the Baals*
> *and they burned incense to*
> *images.*
> *It was I who taught Ephraim to*
> *walk,*
> *taking them by the arms;*
> *but they did not realize*
> *it was I who healed them.*
> *I led them with cords of human*
> *kindness, with ties of love;*
> *I lifted the yoke from their neck*
> *and bent down to feed them (NIV).*

This description could only come from someone who has felt the hurt of rejection. Hosea deeply knew that pain.

15. Messianic Expectations

Hosea, more than any other prophet, portrayed God as a God of unconditional love who was continually wooing Israel to win back her love. This was vividly displayed in Hosea 2:14-23. The love of God was so great that all of Israel's sins and violations could not snuff it out.

Hosea's emphasis on God's unconditional love foreshadowed the focus of Jesus' ministry. Hosea understood the nature of grace. George L. Robinson notes of Hosea, "His book is both a prophecy and a poem; one of the most difficult, but at the same time one of the most evangelical of the Old Testament. This is due not to any special Messianic predictions enunciated, but because he announced centuries in advance 'the new commandment' of the Gospels, and was the first of the seers to grasp the truth that God is love, and that Israel's sin of sins was not to have recognized the love of God. Hosea was thus the St. John of the Old Testament."[47]

Hosea 14 demonstrates the universality and unconditional nature of God's love. He punished Israel so that she would be healed. He destroyed Israel in order to restore her. His love would freely flow to Israel in exile as he anticipated restoring his people to greatness.

16. Important Passage: Hosea 2:14-23

A Marriage Made in Heaven

Therefore I am now going to allure
  her;
I will lead her into the desert
and speak tenderly to her.
There I will give her back her
  vineyards,
and will make the Valley of
  Achor a door of hope.
There she will sing as in the days
  of her youth,
as in the day she came up out of Egypt.

"In that day," declares the Lord,
  "you will call me 'my husband;'
you will no longer call me 'my
  master.'
I will remove the names of the Baals
  from her lips;
no longer will their names be invoked."

"In that day I will make a covenant
  for them
with the beasts of the field and
  the birds of the air
and the creatures that move along
  the ground.

> Bow and sword and battle
> > I will abolish from the land,
> > so that all may lie down in
> > safety.
> I will betroth you to me forever;
> > I will betroth you in
> righteousness and justice,
> > in love and compassion.
> I will betroth you in faithfulness,
> > and you will acknowledge the Lord.
>
> "In that day I will respond,"
> > declares the Lord¬
> "I will respond to the skies,
> and they will respond to the earth;
> > and the earth will respond to the grain,
> the new wine and oil,
> > and they will respond to Jezreel.
> I will plant her for myself in the land;
> > I will show my love to the one I called
> 'Not my loved one.'
> I will say to those called 'Not my People,'
> > You are my people;
> and they will say, 'You are my God'" (NIV).

Introduction.

Almost everyone loves a good love story. I know my wife loves a good love story. She would rather not watch a movie than see one with a sad ending. She likes the storybook ending; she wants people to live happily ever after. *Ladyhawke* is one of our favorite movies. In it a wicked priest who is overcome by jealousy and passion places a curse on two young lovers. The lovers can never touch because by day she becomes a hawk and by night he becomes a wolf. Only at daybreak and sunset are the two able to catch a glimpse of each other as they change into another form. In the end they discover a way to break the curse and they live—

you guessed it—happily ever after.

God also enjoys a story with a happy ending. In fact he de-sires for everyone to experience the "happily ever after." In a sense this is the theme of the Bible—God's mighty acts through history guide humanity to the "happily ever after." Hosea touches on this theme. Because of God's unconditional love for us, he desires for all of us to be happy.

Throughout history God has attempted to display his love for the world. The most radical portrayal of God's love for us is seen in the cross of Jesus. Never has a greater example of un-conditional love been demonstrated. Another example of God's limitless love is expressed through the life of Hosea. In order for Hosea to understand God's love, he needed to experience it in his own life. So God commanded Hosea to take a prostitute as his wife. Hosea knew that his wife would not stay faithful to him. Yet he continued to love her and care for her as if she were faithful. This demonstrated his unconditional love for her.

Likewise God unconditionally loved Israel even though she was continually unfaithful to him. Israel deserved death (which was the Old Testament punishment for marital unfaithfulness), yet time and time again God offered Israel another chance.

In Hosea 2:1-13 God began divorce proceedings against Is-rael. His patience had been stretched to the limit, and it was now time to end his relationship with his wife. His complaints against Israel were many:

Vs. 2, Israel was adulterous and unfaithful.

Vs. 5, She craved the food, water, wool, linen, oil and drink of Baal.

Vs. 8, Israel took silver and gold from Baal, not even acknowledging that Yahweh had provided for her.

Vs. 13, She followed Baal and forgot God.

Israel had reached a state of total depravity. She was lewd and misguided, totally oblivious to her condition.

Because of her actions, Israel must pay the penalty of divorce. God's punishment was just and deserved. He would punish her through a series of events:

Vs. 3, God would strip Israel naked.
Vs. 4, God would discipline Israel.
Vs. 6, God would wall Israel in so that she could not escape to prostitute herself with Baal.
Vs. 9, God would take back his blessings from her.
Vs. 10, He would expose her lewdness.
Vs. 13, God would punish her for her sins.

By the time Hosea reached verse thirteen, he had reached a crescendo. We expect to see an avalanche of punishment come careening down upon Israel. But God's absence once again revealed his presence.

I. The Romance. 2:14-15. The Restoration.
Just as Hosea reached the crescendo in his pronouncement of punishment on Israel, the tempo changed. Instead of punishment, God announced that he was once again going to romance Israel. He called off the divorce. He put on his best clothes, learned the most romantic poetry, bought candy and flowers and courted Israel all over again.

He took Israel back to the wilderness where they first met. God reminded her of how they fell in love the first time. He would "allure her" and "speak tenderly" to her. His concern for her could never die because his love was unconditional.

God would restore Israel to her former glory, but this time he would go even beyond what he did at the beginning. He would rebuild her vineyards and renew his gift of the land to his people. He would change their most dismal disappointments into events of great hope. Hosea used the example from Israel's history when the people of Ai defeated Israel because of Achan's sin (Joshua 7:24). The Valley of Achor was a symbol of great disappointment to Israel. Here Achan and his family were stoned to death because they brought defeat to the nation. Yet this symbol of defeat would become a gateway of hope.

This reminds us of two aspects of God's character. First, we see that God is the giver of all great gifts. Israel had forgotten this. God reminds Israel of their history together, a great history of his mighty actions, which were done for her benefit. Many of the Psalms rehearse these salvation acts to remind Israel of all that God had done. We need to remind ourselves of all of God's saving acts in our own lives. We should take time to meditate on what he has done to make sure we know of his love. As the Psalmist did, we should record these mighty acts of God in verse to be repeated and rehearsed so we may never forget them.

Second, Hosea declares that God is willing to restore us to glory in spite of our rebellious past. This was God's nature in the eighth century BC, the first century AD, and today. Paul reminds us of this in Romans 5:6-8: "You see, at just the right time, when we were still powerless, Christ died for the ungodly. Very rarely will anyone die for a righteous man, though for a good man someone might possibly dare to die. But God demonstrates his own love for us in this: While we were still sinners, Christ died for us" (NIV).

God desires a relationship with us. He romances us in order to restore us to glory—glory as only he can give.

II. The Wedding. 2:16-20. The Realization.

God desired to usher in a new age for Israel. This would be an age where Israel would no longer seek after Baal as her husband, but Yahweh would be her husband. The new age would be so pleasing to Israel that she would totally forget the name of Baal. He would never be mentioned again. She would only desire Yahweh.

This new age was the Messianic age long anticipated by the Hebrew prophets. Israel would be different in this age. She would become everything that God had desired for her to be. She would have security, contentment and peace—the Old Testament concept of *shalom*. God would bless her by giving her peace with the animal kingdom (vs. 18 and Isaiah 11:6-9). God would give her security from other people by keeping her free from war (see

Isaiah 2:4).

Hosea was looking forward to a time in the future for Israel. He knew that this new age was not for the present generation. But as spring followed winter, life would come from death for Israel. Douglas Stuart notes, "Logically, this new relationship initiated by Yahweh in 2:16-17 reflects a time after the substantial punishments represented in the previous verses are complete. The focus is eschatological. After destruction and exile, a remnant of northern Israel will still have a future."[48]

God would marry Israel and care for her as a husband cared for his wife. He would provide for her every need. At the wedding, God offered lavish gifts for his bride to enjoy. These gifts reminded Israel that she was not married to just anyone, but she had given herself to Yahweh—the giver of every great gift. Consider what Israel would receive as a bridal gift:

(1.) *tesedheq*. Righteousness. This is a quality of salvation and deliverance that only God can give. Righteousness is a knowledge that all has been forgiven, and since we are forgiven, we should walk in righteousness. It is the vertical relationship with God that we must all work on. But since we have this vertical relationship with God, it extends horizontally to all our relationships with other people.

(2.) *mishpat*. Justice. Justice is *tesedheq* as it is expressed in relationships. We cannot just concentrate on the vertical relationship and forget the horizontal relationships in which we engage every day. We must act righteously toward others.

(3.) *hesed*. Mercy, loyalty. My Hebrew teacher in seminary, Dr. Emil Scoggins, taught us to translate *hesed* as "grace, mercy, peace". Most translators use the term "steadfast love." It is an unfailing, binding devotion, which keeps a covenant relationship alive. This is God's unconditional love—his consistent good treatment no matter the response.

(4.) *rachamim*. Compassion. This is God's parental attentiveness, which includes protective love and forgiveness and concern for whoever is in need.

(5.) '*emunah*. Faithfulness. Faithfulness can also be seen as truth, reliability, honesty, believability and dependability. Newsome says it is "a consistency in personal relationships that is the basis of all lasting relationships."[49]

The result was that Israel would know God and God would know Israel. After all these gifts from God, he expected only one reciprocal action—acknowledgement. This term, *da ath 'elohim*, is the term used throughout the Old Testament for the consummation of a marriage. Israel should have responded to God out of love because he had loved Israel. In a marriage you do things not because you "have to" but because you "want to." When you perform these little actions of love there is no interest in getting anything in return. You are giving because it is a joy to give. This is the basis of a loving relationship. And we respond to God because he has established a loving relationship with us.

III. The "Happily Ever After." 2:21-23. The Reality.
God is in the business of changing people's lives. He took Israel through a divorce suit, back through courtship, married her and then offered her a happily-ever-after storybook ending. Hosea illustrated this by using a play on words with the name of his children. The name of Hosea's first daughter was *Lo'ruhamah*, which means "not loved." God would transform this despondent child into *Ruhamah*—loved. He named his second son *Lo'ammi* meaning "not my people." God would change him into *Ammi*—my people. These names symbolized the rebellious character of Israel. Now God turned those names on end and demonstrated the enormous change he would bring in Israel's life.

This foreshadowed the way that Jesus would change lives centuries later. Peter announced this change in I Peter 2:9-10: "But you are a chosen people, a royal priesthood, a holy nation, a people belonging to God, that you may declare the praises of him who called you out of darkness into his wonderful light. Once you were not a people, but now you are the people of God; once you had not received mercy, but now you have received mercy" (NIV).

God loves to transform lives. He takes the tragic story and gives it the storybook ending. He desires for everyone to live "happily ever after."

Jose's Tune

I sing of the Love Unconditional.
ruined
shattered
grieved
pained

I sing of the Love Unconditional.
wooed
romanced
courted
loved

I sing of the Love Unconditional.
corrected
devoted
protected
believed

I sing of the Love Unconditional.
changed
restored
accepted
completed

I sing of the Love Unconditional.

I sing
I sing
I sing.
 —G. Steve Kinnard, November 1982

References
Andersen, F. I. and D. N. Freedman. *Hosea*. Anchor Bible. 1980.

Brown, S. L. *The Book of Hosea with Introduction and Notes*. 1932.

Brueggeman, Walter. *Tradition for Crisis*. 1968.

Buss, M. J. *The Prophetic Word of Hosea*. 1969.

Cheyne, T. K. *Hosea with Notes and Introduction*. 1984.

Davies, G. Hosea. New Century Bible Commentary. 1992.

Macintosh, A. A. *Hosea*. International Critical Commentary. 1997.

Mays, J. L. *Hosea*. Old Testament Library. 1974.

Robinson, H. Wheeler. *The Cross of Hosea*. 1959.

_____. *Two Hebrew Prophets*. 1948.

Scott, Melville. *The Message of Hosea*. 1921.

Snaith, Norman H. *Amos, Hosea, and Micah*. 1956.

_____. *Mercy and Sacrifice*. 1953.

Tweedie, A. *A Sketch of Amos and Hosea*. 1916.

Wolff, H. *Hosea*. Hermeneia. 1974.

6

Isaiah Ben Amoz
The Prophet of Holiness

Holy, Holy, holy is the Lord Almighty;
the whole earth is full of his glory.
—Isaiah 6:3

Isaiah carried his religion into his politics, and it was his sense of Yahweh that dictated his attitude to all nations. Assyria might have the most powerful military organization on earth, but Yahweh was stronger than Assyria, and even the rod of His anger, "if she went too far," would find that the God of Israel could protect His own. Still more, then, should Judah have seen that her only true defender and friend was Yahweh. It was safer for her to trust in Him than even to repair her weak and damaged battlements. Not only supreme power was His, but supreme wisdom also. It was worse than useless to exclude Him from the councils of the nation. He was ready to make Himself known, in prophecy and in other ways, and there was no need to adopt any other course than to consult Him under all circumstances. The first thing, the last thing, the only thing for Israel to remember was that He was her God, and she His people.[50]

—*Theodore H. Robinson, OT scholar*

1. Date

Isaiah is a younger contemporary of the prophet Hosea and a contemporary of Micah in the Southern Kingdom. Isaiah prophesied during the last half of the eighth century BC. Isaiah himself records his call as occurring in the year of Uzziah's death (740 BC).

2. Location: Jerusalem, the capital city of the Southern Kingdom of Judah.

3. Purpose

To prepare Judah for the coming judgment of God which would result in the devastation of Jerusalem and exile of its inhabitants. Isaiah also encourages his audience by looking beyond the judgment to a time when the exiles would return to Jerusalem.

4. Theme: "Holy, Holy, Holy is the Lord God of Hosts."

5. Meaning of Name: Isaiah means "the Lord is Salvation."

6. Audience

Chapters 1-39 were written to the people of Judah during the second half of the eighth century. Chapters 40-66 looked forward to the post-exilic Jews in the second half of the sixth century.

7a. Outline:

I. Prophecies Concerning Judah and Jerusalem, 1-12.

II. Oracles of Judgment upon the Nations, 13-23.

III. God's Great Judgments, 24-27.

IV. Prophetic Warnings: True and False Hopes in Zion,

28-35.

V. Jerusalem's Judgment Delayed, 36-39.

VI. The Promise of Divine Deliverance, 40-56:8.

VII. The Promise of God's Universal Kingdom, 56:9-66:24.

7b. Extended Outline.

1:1-12:6—Isaiah's memoirs.

1:1-5:30—Oracles against rebellious Judah
1:1—Superscription
1:2-31—A first series of oracles, which serve as a prologue: God attacks the religious superficiality of Judah.
2:1—A second superscription
2:2-5—The new age for Zion that God will build
2:6-22—The day of the Lord will be a day of judgment
3:1-15—The sins of Jerusalem create anarchy in the land.
3:16-4:1—The reproach of the women of Jerusalem
4:2-6—The restoration of Jerusalem's glory
5:1-7—The allegory of the song of the vineyard
5:8-23—Isaiah speaks out against six sins of Judah: covetousness (8-10), carousing (11-12), mocking God (18-19), moral depravity (20), conceit (21) and bribery (22-23).
5:24-30—God's judgment upon Judah for her sins
6:1-13—The call of Isaiah in the temple of Yahweh
7:1-8:15—Isaiah's memoirs of the Syro-Ephraimite War of 734-733 BC
7:1-9—Isaiah gives the sign of a remnant in the naming of Shearjashub ("a remnant shall return"). He tells Ahaz not to fear the coalition of Syria and Samaria.
7:10-17—The sign of Immanuel ("God with Us") is

offered to Ahaz to strengthen his confidence in Yahweh.
7:18-25—Judgment pronounced
8:1-4—The sign of Maher-shalal-hash-baz ("Quick to
the plunder, quick to the spoil") is the third assurance to
Isaiah.
8:5-10—Oracle of judgment
8:11-22—The memoirs of Isaiah during the war
9:1-7—Oracle about the Messianic king and the future
glory of Galilee
9:8-10:4—The judgment of Ephraim as a lesson for
Judah
10:5-19—Oracle of Woe against Assyria
10:20-23—God will destroy Judah, but a remnant will
survive.
10:24-27—An oracle of promise for Judah
10:27-34—The Assyrians are God's rod of discipline.
11:1-9—Oracle of the future glory of the Messianic king
11:10-16—Oracle of the future glory of the Messianic age
12:1-3—A song of deliverance
12:4-6—A song of thanksgiving

13:1-23:18—Isaiah's oracles against the foreign nations

13:1-22—Oracle against Babylon
14:1-2—Judah's return from exile
14:3-23—A taunt over the death of a Babylonian tyrant
which would precede Judah's return from exile
14:24-27—Oracle against Assyria
14:28-32—Oracle against Philistia
15:1-16:14—Oracle against Moab
17:1-6—Isaiah prophecies against the Syro-Ephraimite
coalition.
17:7-11—Oracle against idolatry
18:1-20:6—Writings concerning the nation of Egypt
18:1-7—Oracle against Egypt

19:1-15—A second oracle against Egypt

20:1-6—A third oracle against Egypt: Isaiah parades naked and barefoot for three years as a sign of what Assyria would do to Egypt.

21:1-10—Oracle against Babylon

21:11-12—Oracle against Edom

21:13-17—Oracle against Arabia

22:1-14—An oracle of warning about Jerusalem's approaching destruction

22:15-25—Oracle against Shebna: Shebna, Hezekiah's household steward, seems to have been a conspirator in the anti-Assyrian plot in 711 BC.

23:1-18—Oracle against Tyre and Sidon

24:1-13—First eschatological section: Isaiah prophesies universal judgment.

24:14-17—A note of deliverance

24:18-23—Second eschatological section: Universal judgment is prophesied.

25:1-5—A psalm of thanksgiving

25:6-10a—The third eschatological section

25:10b-12—An oracle of doom against Moab

26:1-6—A song of victory

26:7-19—An apocalyptic psalm

26:20-27:1—The fourth eschatological section

27:2-11—An apocalyptic poem of deliverance

27:12-13—A concluding oracle of doom and triumph

28:1-35:10—Oracles concerning Judah and Ephraim

28:1-13—Pronouncements against the religious leaders

28:14-22—Pronouncements against the civil leaders

28:23-29—The parable of the farmer: As a farmer, God patterns his business according to a plan.

29:1-8—The future glory of Judah

29:9-24—Oracles against spiritual blindness

30:1-7—Isaiah resists the plan to form an alliance with

Egypt against Assyria in 703 BC.

30:8-17—Isaiah warns against trusting in Egypt

30:18-26—The future prosperity of Judah

30:27-33—Oracle against Assyria

31:1-3—Oracle against Egypt

31:4-9—Oracle against Sennacherib

32:1-8—Judah's future age of justice

32:9-14—Oracle against the complacency of Judah's women

32:15-20—The age when the Spirit is poured out will cause the transformation of all creation.

33:1-24—A prophetic liturgy used in the temple service to demonstrate the evil of Judah

34:1-17—An oracle announcing the end of God's enemies

35:1-10—The restoration of Zion

36:1-39:8—Historical appendix

36:1-22—The attack of Sennacherib upon Jerusalem in 701 BC

37:1-35—King Hezekiah receives counsel from Isaiah about the Assyrian crisis.

37:36-38—The devastation of the army of Sennacherib and the king's death

38:1-22—The illness of Hezekiah and his recovery

39:1-8—Hezekiah welcomes the embassy of Babylon into Jerusalem.

40:1-55:13—The book of comfort for Israel

40:1-11—The pronouncement of the coming of God for those in exile

40:1.2-31—A hymn of praise for the creator of the universe

41:1-42:4—The trial of the nations

42:1-4—The First Servant Song
42:5-17—God's glorious victory
42:18-43:7—Israel is portrayed as a blind and deaf servant
43:8-13—Israel serves as God's witness to the depravity of the nations.
43:14-44:8—The redemption and restoration of Israel
44:9-20—Oracle used to satirize idolatry
44:21-23—The redemption of Israel
44:24-45:13—The commission of Cyrus as Israel's Messiah
45:14-25—The conversion of the nations
46:1-13—Yahweh will make Israel strong
47:1-15—A lament for Babylon
48:1-22—The God of history is Israel's God
49:1-6—The Second Servant Song
49:7-26—The restoration of Israel
50:4-11—The Third Servant Song
51:1-16—God's salvation is forever.
51:17-52:12—God provides salvation for Judah.
52:13-53:12—The Fourth Servant Song: The Song of the Suffering Servant
54:1-17—A Song of Assurance to Israel
55:1-13—A hymn of triumph for Israel's restoration

56:1-66:24—The third section of Isaiah: The oracles looking forward to the restoration of Judah

56:1-8—The blessings of the righteous life
56:9-12—Oracle against corrupt leaders
57:1-13—Oracle against idolatry
57:14-21—A poem of comfort for the righteous
58:1-14—The proper fast
59:1-21—A call to national repentance
60:1-62:12—Hymns to the future glory of Zion

60:1-22—The glory of Jerusalem is restored
61:1-11—The mission of Zion
62:1-12—The future glory of God's people
63:1-6—The divine judgment
63:7-64:12—Israel calls upon Yahweh for vindication.
65:1-25—God will transform Israel.
66:1-24—Conclusion.

8. Memory Work

Isaiah 1:3
The ox knows it owner,
*   and the ass its master's crib;*
but Israel does not know,
*   my people does not understand.*

Isaiah 9:6
For to us a child is born,
*   to us a son is given;*
and the government will be upon
*   his shoulder,*
and his name will be called
*   "Wonderful Counselor, Mighty God,*
Everlasting Father, Prince of Peace."

Isaiah 11:1-3
And the Spirit of the Lord shall
*   rest upon him,*
the spirit of wisdom and
*   understanding,*
the spirit of counsel and might,
*   the spirit of knowledge and the*
*   fear of the Lord.*
And his delight shall be in the fear of the Lord.

Isaiah 25:8
He will swallow up death forever, and the Lord God will wipe away tears from all faces, and the reproach of his people he will take away from all the earth; for the Lord has spoken.

Isaiah 33:5-6
The Lord is exalted, for he dwells
on high;
he will fill Zion with justice and
righteousness;
and he will be the stability of your
times;
abundance of salvation, wisdom,
and knowledge;
the fear of the Lord is his
treasure.

Isaiah 35:8-10
And a highway shall be there,
and it shall be called the Holy Way;
the unclean shall not pass over it,
and fools shall not err therein.
No lion shall be there,
nor shall any ravenous beast come
up on it;
they shall not be found there,
but the redeemed shall walk there.
And the ransomed of the Lord shall
return,
and come to Zion with singing;
everlasting joy shall be upon their
heads;
they shall obtain joy and gladness,
and sorrow and sighing shall flee
away.

Isaiah 40:8
The grass withers, the flower fades;
but the word of our God will stand
forever.

Isaiah 53:4-6
Surely he has borne our griefs
and carried our sorrows;
yet we esteemed him stricken,
smitten by God, and afflicted.
But he was wounded for our
transgressions,
he was bruised for our iniquities,
upon him was the chastisement that
made us whole,
and with his stripes we are healed.
All we like sheep have gone astray;
we have turned every one to his
own way;
and the Lord has laid on him
the iniquity of us all.

Isaiah 55:8-9
For my thoughts are not your
thoughts,
neither are your ways my ways,
says the Lord.
For as the heavens are higher than
the earth,
so are my ways higher than your
ways
and my thoughts than your
thoughts.

Isaih 59:1-2
Behold, the Lord's hand is

*not shortened, that it cannot
save,
or his ear dull, that it cannot hear;
but your iniquities have made a
separation
between you and your God,
and your sins have hidden his face from
you
so that he does not hear.*

9. Special notes
I. Unity of Authorship
Although numerous modern scholars attack the idea that Isaiah wrote the entire book attributed to him, the following considerations support Isaiah's authorship.

(1.) New Testament authors quote from various parts of the book, and they attribute the material to Isaiah.
(2.)The language used in all parts of the book is similar.
(3.) The tradition of Isaianic authorship is at least as old as the second century BC (compare the Dead Sea Scrolls manuscript of Isaiah and the book of Ecclesiasticus 49:17-25).
(4.) The basis for the case against the unity of the book is naturalistic presupposition. In other words, people who deny predictive prophecy also deny that one prophet named Isaiah is responsible for the work.
(5.) The heading of the book in 1:1 quite naturally refers to the entire work.
(6.) There is no external evidence for division.

Modern scholarship fails to believe that the book of Isaiah came from the hand of Isaiah. They identify three distinct Isaiah's written from three different times in history:

First Isaiah, Chapters 1-39. Pre-Exilic to 700 BC. Israel is on a collision course with Yahweh. Judgment is imminent.

Second Isaiah, Chapters 40-55. 550 to 538 BC. "Comfort" is the theme of this section of Isaiah. Isaiah uses the metaphors of a new creation and a new exodus.

Third Isaiah, Chapters 56-66. 537 to 516/515 BC. The people need comfort and correction because the return was not what Second Isaiah had prophesied.

Many differences exist between conservative and liberal scholarship over the unity of Isaiah. We will now consider some of these differences.

In a work like this, we cannot take the time to fully consider the history of criticism of Isaiah; the better introductions to the Old Testament provide this information. Suffice it to say, since Johann C. Doederlein in 1789 argued for a sixth century date of Isaiah 40-66 the floodgate of hypotheses about Isaianic authorship has not closed. Today most biblical students accept the theory of two, possibly three, authors of Isaiah.

Three reasons are given for dating Isaiah 40-66 as post-exilic. We will examine these reasons under these headings: A. Differences in theme and subject matter, B. Differences in language and style, C. Differences in theological ideas, and D. Other considerations.

A. Differences in theme and subject matter.

Critics suggest that the material in Isaiah 40-66 is written to a group of Jews who were suffering in Babylon. The author does not take a predictive stance, but writes as if people were in exile. Critics see it unlikely that Isaiah ben Amoz could write in this style for such a prolonged time.

Critics also contend that it would be impossible for Isaiah to know with such great detail the conditions of the exiles in Babylon. For the material to be written with such accuracy implies a writer with firsthand knowledge of the situation.

In answer to these criticisms, it is interesting to note that liberal scholars were divided in their attempt to disprove the unity of Isaiah. When critical opinions of Isaiah were first expressed, the consensus of scholarship was that Second Isaiah was written from Babylon during the exile. After further study many scholars admitted that the places, geography and cultural situations in Isaiah 40-66 actually suggested a writer who was in Palestine. No reference is given in Isaiah to any location other than Judah or Jerusalem as being the home of the inhabitants of Israel. Although the themes in 40-66 suggest an exilic background, a more literal reading of the prophet places the Jews in the Southern Kingdom of Judah.

The main reason modern scholars reject Isaiah 40-66 as Isaianic is their denial of the legitimacy of predictive prophecy. Could Isaiah ben Amoz in 740 BC have foretold events 150 years before they happened with such accuracy? Could he have seen events so clearly as to name places and mention an unborn Cyrus of Persia as being the anointed shepherd of Israel (44:28; 46:1)? Critics answer, "No." Most of them don't believe in predictive prophecy, and therefore, they reject Isaianic authorship. The literary and theological differences are secondary. Gleason Archer, one of the few Old Testament scholars who upholds the unity of Isaiah, writes:

> By and large, however, the principal architects of the two-Isaiah theory have simply assumed on rationalistic grounds the impossibility of divine revelation in genuinely predictive prophecy."[51]

Either the Bible contains predictive prophecy or it does not. For the higher critic any reference that looks like fulfilled prophecy must be a later interpolation into the text. What about Micah 5:2? Micah predicted the birthplace of the Messiah a full seven centuries before the birth of Jesus? Also consider that a prophet of Judah foretold the name of Josiah a full three centuries before this great king of the reform was born (I Kings 13:2).

Higher criticism not only attacks predictive prophecy in the Bible, it also takes exception to the supernatural miracles recorded in both Testaments including the miracles of Christ. I once had a professor in seminary who attempted to explain away every miracle of Christ. He attacked Jesus turning water into wine as mere trickery and spoke of Jesus walking on the water as an optical illusion. He had an answer for every specific miracle of Jesus. One morning very close to Easter Sunday, this professor startled us by pausing in his lecture to verify the veracity of the resurrection. "If Jesus died and is still dead," he expressly stated, "there is no Christianity!" He went on to say, "Jesus rose from the dead on the third day just as the Bible states." We were stunned. How could he deny every miracle of Jesus and yet, hold so tenaciously to the resurrection? One student asked, "But, Professor, if you can believe the resurrection of Jesus, why can't you believe that he changed water into wine or that he walked on the water? After all, which is more difficult to believe?"

The resurrection is the most central issue in Christianity. Either it happened or it didn't. If not, there is no Christianity. Jesus was a hoax. Let's close shop. If true, then every other thing he said or did becomes gospel—including his miracles. After accepting the resurrection, it is easy to believe that God could predict 700 years in advance the place where his son would be born. If one can accept the virgin birth, one can accept that Isaiah predicted the event (Isaiah 7:14). Once the resurrection is accepted, it is easy to believe Isaiah ben Amoz could have named Cyrus as the anointed shepherd 150 years before his birth.

The second half of Isaiah is not the only section with predictive prophecy; the first half also has references to the future. Modern scholarship would see these references as interpolations into the text by disciples of Isaiah, but can they be dismissed so easily? Isaiah told king Hezekiah not to worry about Sennacherib's march on Jerusalem, and the city was spared by supernatural intervention (37:33-35). Isaiah also foretold the defeat of Damascus by the Assyrians three years before the event and the destruction of Samaria twelve years prior to the event (8:4, 7; 7:16). Other situations were predicted which did not occur until years after Isaiah's death. Isaiah prophesied the fall of Babylon to the Medes and Persians decades before it happened (13:17). He claimed that like Sodom and Gomorrah, Babylon would be so decimated as to be uninhabited (13:19-20). There are also Messianic references in the first half of Isaiah. Must we explain away every single predictive prophecy in the Bible? Liberal scholarship would answer, "Yes." But once predictive prophecy is accepted, then we can accept the unity of the book of Isaiah.

Isaiah 40-66 presupposes that Judah would be taken into captivity by the Babylonians and would struggle with their faith while in exile. Is it not possible that Isaiah ben Amoz saw this captivity coming and penned these chapters to explain to the Hebrews why their Sovereign God was allowing this to occur and to inform them of how God would work through it? The decimation of the Northern Kingdom and the Assyrian march on Jerusalem would have prepared Isaiah for the possibility of Judah's exile. Many verses in chapters 40-66 attempt to place the exile in proper perspective allowing for the sovereignty and love of God (41:26; 42:9, 23; 43:9, 12; 44:7-8). Archer comments:

> Such passages as these make it abundantly plain that the extensive and precise predictions of the future contained in these chapters of Isaiah II were intended to achieve a very special purpose. They were to furnish confirmation that the prophet's message was in fact the message of the one true God, who is absolute Sovereign over the affairs of men; that it was by His decree rather than because of the might of Babylon that the covenant nation would be carried off in captivity. Only through the powerful encouragement of fulfilled prediction would the future generation of exiles summon up the courage to return to Palestine, even after the permission of the new Persian government had been granted.[52]

B. Differences in language and style

Opponents of the one-author theory of Isaiah point to stylistic differences between chapters 1-39 and 40-66. New phrases and images are used to replace some of the outmoded ideas in the first part. The style of Isaiah ben Amoz is said to be terse and compact, whereas, his "mimic" writes with lyrical charm and use of emotional images. Critics point to the fact that in 40-66 there is a catalog of words not used in 1-39.

One major objection to the source-critical school's approach to the Bible is that they propose to know the author of a source because of his style and language, they then deny his authorship because of certain stylistic inconsistencies. In other words, they build their straw man and then tear him apart. They fail to recognize the close verbal agreements between Isaiah 1-39 and 40-66.

Isaiah could have changed style and vocabulary because of a change in the political-religious environment in Judah or simply because of his own maturation. By studying the works of C.S. Lewis, we can detect a marked difference between Lewis' writings as a young man and those of his later years. Part of the diversity occurs because as a youth Lewis was an atheist, and later during his days as a professor at Oxford his friend, J. R. R. Tolkien, introduced him to Christianity. Changes in his style also occur because he wrote many different types of literature from children's books to practical theology and from literary criticism to science fiction.

Writers grow over time. Their writing style changes. Their vocabulary changes. Their syntax changes. Don't we all know that over time writers can change from writing short, quick, exact sentences of three or four words into writers that string out long sentences full of clauses and phrases that are joined together by prepositions and conjunctions that look like a paragraph, (as I have just demonstrated)?

We also must consider that many stylistic similarities exist between the first and second halves of Isaiah. Both sections refer to God as "the Holy One of Israel." Although this term appears only five times outside of Isaiah, it appears twelve times in the first section and fourteen times in the second section of Isaiah. This title proposes a unifying theological theme found throughout Isaiah—the theme of the holiness of God.

C. Differences in theological ideas.

Critics claim differences in the theology of chapters 1-39 and 40-66. The earlier portions stress the holiness of God and the later half portrays God's uniqueness and eternal nature. The first half places Yahweh above all other gods, and the latter half describes Yahweh as the sole deity as if no other gods existed. The concept of the remnant is different in that the first half sees the remnant left behind in Jerusalem and the second half sees them in exile about to be released back into Jerusalem. Chapters 1-39 give a description of the Messianic king and 40-66 describe the suffering servant.

Is it not possible that Isaiah simply switched gears as he turned to pen chapters 40-66? Could there not have been a break of weeks, months or years, which led him to write in a slightly different vein? We know of at least a twenty-year gap in Isaiah's writing activity. He could have been describing real events in chapter 1-39 and then turned to a more idealistic picture of Israel in chapters 40-66. Critics see points in the first section where Isaiah describes future events as if they had happened (5:13ff.; 9:1ff.; 23:1-14). Could he not have continued in that style for a lengthy time to encourage and comfort God's people? Isaiah did not need to repeat the warning of exile in 40-66 since he thought of the exile as beginning within his lifetime.

These theological differences can be viewed as Isaiah's attempt to broaden themes, which he discussed in the early sections of his work. The Messianic king is also mentioned in Isaiah 55:3, although Isaiah prefers to emphasize the suffering servant motif in the second section. We must also consider the commonality of the themes in Isaiah 40-66 with the work of Micah. Perhaps Isaiah was borrowing from Micah's work?

No one has ever pointed out any genuine contradictions in the two sections of Isaiah. If they exist, where are they? No critic has ever demonstrated that those thematic differences, which do occur, could not possibly be the result of Isaiah changing his emphasis because of the wicked reign of Manasseh. In considering all the evidence postulated by the critics, R.K. Harrison concludes, "The unfortunate fact remains that divisive theories of the composition of Isaiah are strictly a matter of assumption rather than of factual proof."[53]

D. Other Considerations.

Gleason Archer in his A Survey of the Old Testament gives five other proofs for the Isaianic authorship of Isaiah 40-66.[54] These are considered in the following:

(1.) The New Testament writers viewed the entirety of Isaiah as being penned by Isaiah ben Amoz. Whenever the New Testament writers quote from Isaiah 40-66 and mention the author, they give credit to Isaiah of Jerusalem (Mt. 12:17-18; Lk. 3:4; Acts 8:28; Rom. 10:16, 20; John 12:38-41).

(2.) If a Deutero-Isaiah did exist, then why were his name, city, occupation, family and biographical material not recorded? As early as 1964, J. A. Alexander pointed out that it would be unique in literary history for a writer to produce such a work of genius without leaving any stamp of his personality on it.[55] Harrison mentions that almost without exception the Hebrews required the name of the prophet for a prophetic oracle to be accepted as Scripture.[56]

(3.) The linguistic evidence favors Isaiah 40-66 being written from Palestine before the exile. If it were written in Babylon after the exile or in Palestine after the exile, we would expect to find Babylonian terms and a mixing of Aramaic and Hebrew. This is what we find in Ezra and Nehemiah who returned from the exile to Palestine. Isaiah is written in a pure, flowing Hebrew.

(4.) Archer points to Isaiah 13:1 as a "serious embarrassment to the theory of an exilic Deutero-Isaiah."[57] This text is attributed to Isaiah ben Amoz and is a prophecy of the downfall of Judah at the hands of the Babylonians. At this time the Babylonians were subjects of the Assyrian state, yet Isaiah foresaw their rise to power and future downfall (Is. 13:17). If Isaiah could predict this event, why could he not also pen chapters 40-66?

(5.) The second half of Isaiah contains verses similar to material found in other seventh-century pre-exilic prophets, namely, Zephaniah, Nahum and Jeremiah.

Modern scholarship chops up the book of Isaiah to the point of making it unreadable for the novice Bible student. The uninitiated could not possibly pick up Isaiah and discern that chapters 40-66 were from another author. Yet higher critics would say that this fact is accepted beyond dispute. Modern scholarship has gone so far as to make almost every oracle and saying in Isaiah uncertain. Klaus Koch upholds the view of diverse authorship of Isaiah, but he has pointed out how the critics have cut Isaiah to pieces with their scissors of scholarship. Koch writes:

> How can we chisel out the original rock of Isaiah? Unfortunately the results arrived at by individual scholars differ widely. Since modern literary criticism has not yet worked out its methods in a complete and comprehensive way, criticism of this kind rests more on the subjective feeling of the interpreter than on provable textual facts—and this is especially true in the case of the prophetic books ... And where authenticity is concerned, I prefer to trust the transmitted text too much rather than too little.[58]

II. Other Special Note in Isaiah.
A. Major Predictive Themes in Isaiah:
  1. The fall of Samaria
  2. The fall of Jerusalem
  3. The exile
  4. The restoration of a righteous remnant
  5. The coming of the Messiah
  6. The establishment of the Messianic kingdom

B. Isaiah and Evangelism
  Isaiah understood that God was concerned with the totality of humanity and not just with his covenant people, Israel, although Israel held a special relationship with Yahweh, and with that uniqueness came special privilege and special responsibility.

Isaiah is one of the first evangelistic prophets. He speaks of God working through Israel to bring the whole world to salvation. God used both Israel and foreign nations as instruments to prepare people's hearts to know him and ultimately to receive his son into the world. Theodore H. Robinson writes:

> Isaiah felt, like Amos before him, that Yahweh was concerned with the fortunes of the whole human race, and not merely with those of Israel. Thus he developed a genuine philosophy of history, and conceived all events to be subordinated to the working out of a single sublime plan. That plan is itself the vindication and illustration of supreme moral laws, which to him are summed up in the character of Yahweh.[59]

Yahweh had acted for the good of Israel and for the good of all humanity. Notice Isaiah 49:5-6:

> *And now the Lord says—*
> *he who formed me in the womb*
> *to be his servant*
> *to bring Jacob back to him*
> *and gather Israel to himself,*
> *for I am honored in the eyes of the*
> *Lord*
> *and my God has been my*
> *strength.*
>
> *He says:*
> *"It is too small a thing for you to be*
> *my servant*
> *to restore the tribes of Jacob*
> *and bring back those of Israel I*
> *have kept.*
> *I will also make you a light for the*
> *Gentiles,*

that you may bring my salvation
to the ends of the earth."

God has blessed Israel as his cherished people, and in doing so
has made her history the key to the world's history.

10. Historical Context

Isaiah prophesied during the reigns of the Judean kings Uzziah, Jotham, Ahaz and Hezekiah. His ministry began during the
year that King Uzziah died. This would place the beginning of
his work in 742 BC. Since Isaiah records the death of Sennach
erib of Assyria in Isaiah 37:37-38, we can assume he was mar-
tyred after his death in 681 BC. Thus, Isaiah's ministry could have
spanned six decades.[60] Tradition continues the ministry of Isaiah
into the reign of Manasseh, Hezekiah's successor, depicting Isaiah's martyrdom by being sawed in two inside a hollow log (see
Heb. 11:37).

As a court prophet Isaiah had a close relationship with the
kings of Judah. To understand Isaiah's writings we must have
knowledge of the kings whom he served. The first king mentioned in Isaiah 1:1 is Uzziah (783-742). Uzziah is also known as
Azariah in the Old Testament text. He was a contemporary of
Jereboam II (786-746). The conditions that abounded in Samaria
during this time also prevailed in Judah, with the exception that
economic conditions were not quite as favorable because Judah
did not have as easy an access to trade as her northern counter-
part.

Uzziah took the throne of Judah at the age of sixteen, thrust
into the role of king by the murder of his father Amaziah. He
took advantage of the weakness of the Assyrians to expand the
borders of Judah both south and east by carrying out military
campaigns against the Arabs, Ammonites and Philistines. He
was able to reclaim land for Judah all the way to the port of Solomon in the Gulf of Aqabah. His reign brought a resurgence of
prosperity to Judah that tended to widen the disparity between
the rich and the poor just as had occurred in Samaria.

With all the good King Uzziah had done for the nation of Judah, his life ended on a sad note. Because Uzziah became puffed up with pride, he attempted to take over the role of the priest and enter the temple of God to perform priestly functions. God struck Uzziah with leprosy and he was unable to ever return to the temple or to his palace. He lived in isolation for the rest of his days sharing the throne with his son Jotham in the year 750 (II Kings 14:21-22; 15:1-7; II Chron. 26:1-23).

Jotham (750-730) continued in the steps of his father placing a high priority on military strength and aggressive building projects within the city of Jerusalem. He seems to have shared the joy of economic stability that Uzziah enjoyed.

Ahaz (735-715) inherited the throne from Jotham just as Tiglath-Pileser III of Assyria was making plans to campaign in upper Syria and Palestine. In 734 King Rezin of Damascus and King Pekah of Samaria invaded Judah in an attempt to either compel Ahaz to join their forces or place someone on the throne who would. This event is recorded in II Kings 16 and II Chronicles 28 as the Syro-Ephraimitic War of 734.

In an effort to save his kingdom, Ahaz appealed to Tiglath-Pileser III for help. The Assyrian monarch already had his eye on Rezin and Pekah. He responded by destroying both Damascus and Samaria, taking the city of Samaria into exile in 722 BC. The losses to Judah during this struggle were costly. Isaiah advised King Ahaz to disregard the threat of Damascus and Samaria and to trust in God. He also protested the alliance of Judah with Assyria. Isaiah proved to be right as Ahaz became a puppet king to the Assyrian empire. Ahaz went so far as to request blueprints for the construction of an altar that was an exact replica of the pagan altar of worship of the Assyrian god Asshur. This altar was to be placed in the Temple in Jerusalem beside the altar of Yahweh. If that were not enough, Ahaz even offered his own son as a sacrifice (II Kings 16 and II Chronicles 28).

Hezekiah (715-697) came into power during a whirlwind. Yet Hezekiah gave his heart to God and with his strong leadership he attempted a reform of the political and religious climate in

Jerusalem (II Kings 18-20 and II Chronicles 29-32). He removed the pagan altars and idols from the temple area and returned to the more orthodox worship of Yahweh. He celebrated a Passover in Jerusalem, which reminded the people of the days of Solomon. His reformation attempted to touch every area of Judean life and even reached beyond the borders of Judah to the expatriates of now-fallen Samaria.

When Sargon II of Assyria died and Sennacherib ascended to his throne in 705 BC, Merodach-baladan of Babylon attempted to rebel against Assyrian rule. Against the advice of Isaiah, who always counseled the kings to avoid foreign alliances, Hezekiah received a Babylonian delegation into Jerusalem in hopes of breaking away from Assyria. At this time all of the vassal kingdoms around Assyria with the exception of Ekron began to rebel against her control. Padi, the king of Ekron, was taken captive by the rebel kingdoms and imprisoned in Jerusalem by Hezekiah. With the possibility of Egypt entering the arena against the Assyrians, Hezekiah was hopeful to break the hold of Assyria once and for all.

Sennacherib was not happy with these developments. In response he swept through Palestine with fire and sword. His records state that he captured forty-six cities in Judah as he marched toward the prize, Jerusalem. His march on Jerusalem ended with a siege, which was spoiled by God's intervention. Although Sennacherib was unable to defeat Jerusalem and complete his campaign, he was able to subdue Hezekiah and extract heavy tribute payments from Judah. Hezekiah served the rest of his reign as a vassal of the Assyrian empire.

In 681 the great Assyrian monarch, Sennacherib was murdered. His son, Esarhaddon, inherited his throne. He had to fight off many rivals for this seat of power over the vast Assyrian kingdom. Once his position was secure, he turned his attention to the west. Egypt once again was stirring up trouble in Palestine for the Assyrians. Assyria marched into Egypt defeating the forces of Pharaoh Taharqa and occupying Lower Egypt. In a successive campaign on Egypt in 669, Esarhaddon died and his son,

Ashurbanipal, took over the campaign. Ashurbanipal was successful in conquering Thebes in 663. The loss of this ancient city, the cultural and political heart of Egypt, was a great blow to the Egyptians.

Hezekiah's son, Manasseh, (687-642) succeeded his father to the throne in Jerusalem just as the Assyrian nation was reaching the zenith of its power. Even the Assyrian monarch must have been surprised at how energetically Hezekiah's son embraced their policy and control. Manasseh brought to Judah a reign of terror unmatched by any other Judean monarch (II Kings 21:1-18). He rebuilt the altars to foreign gods, which Hezekiah had torn down. He offered his own son upon those altars, accepting the worship of the occult in Jerusalem. Manasseh ruled with an iron rod murdering those who would not submit to his power. Tradition states that he murdered the prophet Isaiah. No other king ruled as long or as treacherously as did Manasseh. His reign spawned a time of silence in the prophets of Israel, a time that lasted for three-quarters of a century.

The majority of Manasseh's reign occurred during the height of Assyrian power. Manasseh passed his crown to his son, Amon, who ruled for only two years (642-640). Amon continued the tradition of his father, wreaking havoc in the religious and political environs of Judah. Conspirators assassinated him and then the state executed those conspirators (II Kings 21:19-26). Manasseh's son, Josiah, gained the throne at the young age of eight. Although at first he was just a puppet king for his elderly advisers, Josiah grew to become a great king of reform for the nation of Judah.

Isaiah 40-55

Jerusalem fell to the Babylonian army in 597 BC. Nebuchadnezzar deported the best of the population of Judah to Babylon. Once in exile, many Jews followed Jeremiah's advice and settled into the Babylonian community, accepting their place in exile. Others separated themselves from their conquerors and lived in anticipation of the day in which they would return to their homeland. Isaiah 40-55 offers comfort for the Jews in exile in the land of Babylon.

11. The Person

Although the biographical facts about Isaiah are sketchy, we do know some facts concerning his life. He was a native of the city of Jerusalem and the son of Amoz. Amoz seems to have been from an influential family in Jerusalem with some social and political standing. Since Isaiah's call in Isaiah 6:1-8 took place in the temple where only the priests were allowed to enter, it is safe to assume that Isaiah was a part of the priesthood and came from a family of priests. Isaiah had a close relationship with the ruling class, and even though his relationship with King Ahaz was strained at best, he was a close adviser and confidante of King Hezekiah. Because he served as an adviser to kings, it seems that Isaiah was a part of the court prophets and was privy to information about both international and domestic affairs.

His time of influence was lengthy. Isaiah 1:1 demonstrates that he served off and on for over 40 years under the reign of three different kings: Jotham (740-733), Ahaz (733-714) and Hezekiah (714-696). He was able to witness the Syro-Ephraimite War of 733, the fall of Samaria in 722, and the march of Assyria on Jerusalem in 710. He probably survived into the reign of Manasseh, witnessing the death of Sennacherib in 681 BC. Tradition states that Isaiah was murdered by being cut in two during the bloody reign of Manasseh.

Isaiah was a prophet with a family. Although we rarely think of the prophets as being married and having children, Isaiah 8:3 mentions Isaiah's wife and child, "Then I went to the prophetess, and she conceived and gave birth to a son. And the Lord said to me, name him *Maher-Shalal-Hash-Baz*." We do not know the name of Isaiah's wife, but we know she was a prophetess. Perhaps Isaiah and his wife worked together as a team to lead the people of Judah.

Their choice of following God affected their children's lives. Both of their sons were given symbolic names. The name of Isaiah's first son was *Shear-Jashub*, which means "a remnant will return." At the Lord's direction he named his second son *Maher-Shalal-Hash-Baz* meaning "quick to the plunder, swift to the spoil." Isaiah and his prophetess wife knew that their children were to be dedicated to God. They saw themselves and their children as instruments to be used by God. Isaiah 18:8 states, "Here am I, and the children the Lord has given me. We are signs and symbols in Israel from the Lord Almighty, who dwells on Mount Zion."

A group of disciples followed Isaiah. Isaiah might have led a prophetic school for young men and women to train them in the ministry (and his wife could also have provided leadership for this school). Isaiah 8:16 notes:

"Bind up the testimony
and seal up the law among my
disciples."

Knowing the hypocrisy and impurity of the priesthood around Jerusalem, Isaiah might have seen a prophetic guild as a means of purifying Judah once and for all. It is to this loyal group of disciples that we owe credit for saving and editing the oracles of Isaiah.

Isaiah was willing to go to great lengths to reveal God's message to his audience. Although his prophetic gestures seem slight when compared to Ezekiel's, he took risks to communicate his message. At one point he took a huge scroll and wrote upon it Maher-shalal-hash-bash to announce that Damascus and Samaria were quick spoil for the nation of Assyria.

Isaiah 20 depicts the most radical gesture that Isaiah made as a prophet. Here the Lord asks Isaiah to go naked and barefoot before his people as a sign that the Egyptians will be taken into captivity by the Assyrians stripped and naked. Isaiah is said to have done this for three years.

Then the Lord said, "Just as my servant Isaiah has gone stripped and barefoot for three years, as a sign and portent against Egypt and Cush, so the king of Assyria will lead away stripped and barefoot the Egyptian captives and Cushite exiles, young and old, with buttocks bared—to Egypt's shame" (Isaiah 20:3-4).

With our Western minds it is difficult to understand how God could ask anyone to perform this type of gesture. Isaiah was a man with a family, both a wife and kids. It must be remembered however, that Isaiah's culture was very different from ours. To see someone parade around naked and barefoot would not have been taken sexually. It was the symbol of complete and utter shame. The Assyrians led their captives into exile stripped and barefoot, linked together by chains, which were joined from one person to the next by placing a hook in the buttocks of the captives. They were literally stripped of all dignity. This shame would be even more pronounced for the Israelites because they were the only group in the Middle East who practiced circumcision. They carried not only their own personal shame, but also the shame of the nation. Is it not amazing that Isaiah would voluntarily take upon himself this shame? Perhaps this explains why Isaiah could write so powerfully about the suffering Messiah who would shame himself for the sins of the world.

As we have just stated, Isaiah suffered for his ministry. Even at the time of his call in Isaiah 6 he was warned that he would preach to people who would not listen to him. He was unpopular with Ahaz because he openly opposed the King's alliance with the Assyrians. Ahaz was a man of compromise, and Isaiah was a man of conviction. Sparks flew as these two men debated the affairs of state.

Isaiah enjoyed more popularity at the court of King Hezekiah. Isaiah influenced Hezekiah in his reforms, although the text does not tell us exactly how Isaiah responded to them. It was sad for Isaiah to have lived during the reign of Manasseh and to be forced to watch all of the reforms of Hezekiah swept away by one godless man. Isaiah's opposition to Manasseh's wickedness led to his death. The martyrdom of Isaiah fortified the disciples of the first century as they had to face rulers like Nero and Domitian, who were just as ruthless and godless as Manasseh.

Scholars generally divide Isaiah's writings between four particular time periods:

A. The first period, the Early Ministry, began with the death of Uzziah and lasted until the outbreak of the Syro-Ephraimitic War between the years 747 and 735 (Isaiah 2-5). This period coincides with the reign of King Jotham, a time of luxury and prosperity for Judah. These writings are reminiscent of Amos and Hosea because they rebuke the wealthy landowners and plead the cause of the common man. Isaiah became a social critic who attempted to awaken sentiments of justice in the lives of his hearers.

B. The second period of writing comes from the time of the Syro-Ephraimitic War between 734-732 (Isaiah 7-9). During this time of threat to Judah, Isaiah advised Ahaz to resist the alliance with the Assyrians and trust in Yahweh for deliverance. Perhaps as a result of Ahaz's rejection of his advice, Isaiah entered a period of silence, which lasted for a number of years (Isaiah 8:16-22). During this time Isaiah entrusted his word to his disciples.

C. Between the second and third period more than 20 years elapsed, a retreat from public ministry (734-715). Isaiah continued his ministry during these years, although no writings have survived from this time. The third period, the Middle Ministry, occurred during the anti-Assyrian rebellion during 713-711 (Isaiah 10-23). Isaiah counseled Hezekiah that rebellion by Judah would result in their devastation by Assyria. During this period Isaiah walked naked and barefoot for three years to symbolize how the Egyptians would be led into captivity.

D. The fourth period, the Later Ministry, began after the anti-Assyrian rebellion and the death of Sennacherib and lasted until the siege of Jerusalem, 705-701 (Isaiah 28-32; 36-39). Isaiah responded to the crisis in Judah, which was instigated by Hezekiah's defiance of Assyria. Isaiah again suggests to Hezekiah that his only hope of thwarting the Assyrian advance is to trust in God. Any covenant with Babylon or Egypt against the Assyrians would be a "covenant with death." When Hezekiah grew troubled over the peril of Jerusalem, Isaiah responded by promising deliverance for the city.

12. The Call
Isaiah 6:1-8.

*In the year of King Uzziah's death I saw the Lord Yah-
weh seated on a high throne; his train filled the sanctuary;
above him stood seraphs, each one with six wings: two to
cover its face, two to cover its feet and two for flying.
And they cried out one to another in this way:
"Holy, holy, holy is Yahweh Sabaoth.
His glory fills the whole earth."
The foundations of the threshold shook with the voice
of the one who cried out, and the Temple was filled with
smoke. I said: "What a wretched state I am in! I am lost,
for I am a man of unclean lips and I live among a people of
unclean lips, and my eyes have looked at the King, Yahweh
Sabaoth."
Then one of the seraphs flew to me, holding in his
hand a live coal, which he had taken from the altar with
a pair of tongs. With this he touched my mouth and said:
'See now, this has touched your lips, your sin is taken
away, your iniquity is purged.'
Then I heard the voice of the Lord saying: "Whom
shall I send? Who will be our messenger?"
I answered, "Here I am, send me."*

I. Isaiah 6:1-4. Divine Manifestation. Adoration.

Isaiah received his call to the ministry in 740 BC, the year of
King Uzziah's death. Being a part of a priestly family, Isaiah had
access to the temple. On one occasion while he was meditating
in the temple, he experienced a theophany much as Moses had
experienced in the wilderness when he was called. Although Israel had envisioned Yahweh as sitting upon his throne (the ark
of the covenant) in many of her Psalms, Isaiah saw what others
had only dreamed of seeing. For Isaiah, the curtain of the Holy of
Holies was pulled aside and he saw Yahweh enthroned upon the

ark of the covenant floating in the air, high and lifted up, and his robe filled the temple. This single event molded Isaiah into the prophet of God's holiness.

The "seraphim" accompanied God. A seraph means "burning one," and these angel-like creatures surrounded Yahweh pronouncing his holiness. With a pair of wings they covered their faces because they were not able to gaze at the glory of God. With a pair of wings they covered their feet that euphemistically means they covered their nakedness. This symbolized their humility as they covered their shame before the God of creation. With their third set of wings they flew around God and fulfilled their purpose—to praise his holiness.

The seraphim pronounced, "Holy, holy, holy is the Lord Almighty." This is the superlative form of holiness. They continued to pronounce this so that it might never be forgotten. Yahweh was supremely holy. No other god could stand in his presence. Holy meant separate or set apart. God was different from man. He was as far removed from them as the heavens were from the earth. Yet the Holy Other had come to dwell among his people. His presence now resided within the temple. And he had chosen Isaiah to tell Judah that his holiness was with them.

Isaiah was unable to shake this image of God from his mind. His oracles are filled with testaments to God's holiness. Because he understood God's holiness, he understood that as long as Israel worshiped God and believed in him they would have no fear. He lived his life as a symbol of worship and adoration to the God who had revealed his holiness to him.

We should also take time to contemplate the greatness of God. How many superlatives can you think of to describe God's character? In what ways do you see him as being separate, different, unlike humans? How thankful are you for those differences? The more we contemplate the holiness of God, the more clearly we see ourselves. Right now, take a minute and meditate upon this sentence: "Holy, Holy, Holy is the Lord Almighty."

II. Isaiah 6:5. Protestation of Weakness. Confession.

After seeing God's holiness, Isaiah began to think about himself. This was a normal reaction to seeing the greatness of God. Often when the prophets were called they would protest their weaknesses. This was true of Moses as well as Jeremiah. Isaiah had just seen perfect holiness, so he thought about his own impurity. Seeing God was like seeing a fresh blanket of snow that covers the ground and leaves everything white and beautiful. It was like seeing a newborn baby who is perfect, fresh and lovely. Yet next to the image of holiness, Isaiah's impurity was very obvious.

This happens to us at times as well. It can happen when we spend time in the Scriptures looking at the life of Jesus and comparing ourselves to him. It can happen in a worship service when the singing, prayer and preaching move us to see God and to see ourselves as we really are. Sometimes a walk in the woods can help us reflect on the glory of God's creation and how small we are compared to the vastness of the universe and the greatness of God. We might talk to another disciple whose zeal or faith is so great that it reminds us of how much we need to grow.

We need these times of realization. It is only by recognizing our weaknesses that we change. Isaiah confessed his impurity to God and that opened the door for God to make a difference in Isaiah's life. God loves it when we admit our faults and are honest about our weaknesses. God glories in weakness. The Apostle Paul had a thorn in his flesh that he continually asked God to take away, but God refused (II Cor. 12). God's grace was sufficient for Paul. Through this weakness, God was able to show Paul and others that it was his power that made Paul great. When we confess our weaknesses, we are giving God an avenue to work powerfully in our lives. Weaknesses can become strengths. The God of Holiness can turn our weaknesses into strengths.

III. Isaiah 6:6-7. Purification. Forgiveness.

Isaiah was in a precarious situation when he stood before Yahweh. He knew God's presence had the power to change people's direction in life because he knew the story of Moses. He also knew that God's presence had the power to kill because he knew the story of Uzzah (II Sam. 6:1-11). Also, the story of King Uzziah was a reminder of God's ability to discipline people as he struck Uzziah with leprosy when he entered the temple without authorization (II Chr. 26:16-21). But God's presence also had the power to heal and to purify. This is what Isaiah experienced.

God has the power to change life once and for all. If we put ourselves in the presence of God, we can be different. There is no need to go on committing the same sins over and over. Lasting change can come from having a relationship with God. This change comes from the power of forgiveness.

IV. Isaiah 6:8. Vocation. Service.

Because God purified Isaiah, Isaiah was compelled to serve God. Forgiveness comes before service. Once grace is understood and accepted, the lifestyle of discipleship can be lived. If discipleship comes before grace, then all that is experienced is painful legalism. Forgiveness motivates us to live fully and wholeheartedly for God. Isaiah's vision of God prompted him to serve God wholeheartedly. When we understand who God is, it allows us to understand who we are and who God wants us to be. This understanding leads to service.

THE WHIRLWIND ROAD

The Muses wrapped in mysteries of light
Came in a rush of music on the night;
And I was lifted wildly on quick wings,
And borne away into the deep of things.
The dead doors of my being broke apart;
A wind of rapture blew across the heart;
The inward song of worlds rang still and clear;
I felt the Mystery the Muses fear;
Yet they went Smartening on the ways untrod,
And hurled me breathless at the feet of God.

I felt faint touches of the Final Truth—
Moments of trembling love, moments of youth.
A vision swept away the human wall;
Slowly I saw the meaning of it all—
Meaning of life and time and death and birth,
But cannot tell it to the men of Earth.
I only point the way, and they must go
The whirlwind road of song if they would know.

—Edwin Markham

13. Structure and Form

Isaiah spoke with a unique voice. His use of language was fluid and powerful. He attracted attention by rebuking and criticizing his audience, then drawing them back with encouragement and hope. His prophetic oracles were some of the most powerful ever to have been uttered. He acquired a divine ability to see the political crisis at hand and evaluate it in terms of God's movement in Israel. Isaiah's prophetic oracles are in a class of their own.

The Hebrew text of Isaiah on the whole has been well preserved through the years. The Qumran (Dead Sea) scrolls contained two Isaiah manuscripts one of which was complete (IQIsa). Although this text differed from the Massoretic text in parts, the variations are minimal. The discovery of the Isaiah manuscripts in the Qumran caves has become one of the greatest textual discoveries in history.

14. Theology
A. Judgment for Judah

Like the other eighth-century prophets, God directed Isaiah to proclaim judgment on his people. God had blessed Judah beyond all the other nations of the earth. Not only had he guided her through history, but also he had established Jerusalem as his holy city where his presence dwelt. But Judah lived as if she were not cognizant of God's blessings:

Sons have I reared and brought up,
but they have rebelled against me.
The ox knows its owner,
and the ass its master's crib;
but Israel does not know,
my people does not understand (Isaiah 1:2-3).

Instead of being a center of justice, Jerusalem was the center of injustice. The home of the faithful was full of unbelief. Her idolatry was second only to her pride. Isaiah 30:12-14 reads:

Therefore thus says the Holy One of Israel,
Because you despise this word,
and trust in oppression and perverseness,
and rely on them;
therefore this iniquity shall be to you
like a break in a high wall, bulging
out, and about to collapse,
whose crash comes suddenly, in an instant;
and its breaking is like that of a potter's vessel
which is smashed so ruthlessly
that among its fragments not a sherd is found
with which to take fire from the hearth,
or to dip up water out of the cistern.

As Samaria fell because of her sin, God was preparing a nation to rise up against Judah and purge sin from her ranks.

The long list of Judah's sins condemned her. Isaiah exposed these sins in his oracles. Sins like:

Idolatry: 2:8-9, 20-22; 10:10-11; 17:7-11; 29:15-16; 30:22; 31:7; 40:18-20; 41:21-24; 42:17; 44:9-20; 45:15-21; 46:1-7; 48:5; 57:1-13.
Injustice: 3:13-15; 10:1-4; 16:3-5; 33:13-16; 58:1-21; 59:1-19; 61:1-4.
Superficiality of religion: 1:10-20; 30:9-11; 43:22-24.
Pride: 2:9-17; 3:16-17; 9:8-9; 10:12-13; 14:13-14; 16:6-7; 23:9; 25:10-11; 47:5-7.

Six sins: covetousness 5:9-10; carousing 5:11-12; mocking God 5:18-19; moral depravity 5:20; conceit 5:21; bribery 5:22-23.
Lack of knowledge/wisdom: 1:3; 5:13; 27:11; 42:18-25.
Moral decay: 9:18-20; 64:5-7; 65:1-7.
Corrupt leaders: 9:13-17; 28:14-22; 56:9-10.
Corrupt religious leaders: 28:1-13; 29:9-12.
Drunkenness: 28:1-8.
Lack of trust: 30:1-7; 30:8-17; 31:1-3; 65:1-7.
Complacency of Judah's women: 32:9-14.

Isaiah was a keen observer of the sins of Judah. He understood God's holiness and knew God's anger over these sins. Because Judah had wandered away from her God, she would now have to face his anger as Israel to the north had faced it.

B. God is Faithful.

If God were to destroy Jerusalem, how would the Hebrew faith survive? Many critics of Isaiah asked this question. Isaiah responded by stressing God's faithfulness. God would punish Judah not because he was vindictive, but because of his love. He would not leave Judah in ruin. If God raised up Israel once, he could do so again. In fact, that is exactly what he would do. Jerusalem would rise out of her ashes to become a righteous city under the rule of a new king (1:26-27).

> *I will turn my hand against you*
> > *and will smelt away your dross as with lye*
> > *and remove your entire alloy.*
> *And I will restore your judges as at the first,*
> > *and your counselors as at the beginning.*
> *Afterward you shall be called the city of righteousness,*
> > *the faithful city.*
> > *In this faithful city a new standard will prevail—the*
> *standard of faith, justice, and righteousness:*
>
> *Behold, I am laying in Zion for a foundation—*

> *a stone, a tested stone*
> *a precious cornerstone, of a sure foundation:*
> *He who believes will not be in haste.*
> *And I will make justice the line,*
> *and righteousness the*
> *plummet (Isaiah 28:16-17).*

Isaiah presented numerous images of the future glory of Israel as a means of declaring the faithfulness of God. God would punish Jerusalem for her sins. Yet out of the ashes of Jerusalem's destruction, God would restore Israel's glory and create greater glory in her future than in her past. Following is a partial list of what Jerusalem would become:

1:26 "the city of righteousness"
1:26 "the faithful city"
18:7 "Mount Zion, the place of the name of the Lord of Hosts"
25:6 "the mountain of the Lord of hosts"
26:1 "a strong city"
29:1, 2, 7 "The city 'Ariel' or 'hero'"
30:29 "The rock of Israel"
52:1 "the Holy city"

Isaiah 40-55: Good News for the Exiles

The material found in these chapters was written with a view toward a time when the Jews of Jerusalem would be in exile. Isaiah tried to comfort those of Jerusalem (both those in the eighth century who like Isaiah accepted God's judgment upon Jerusalem and those in the sixth century who were in exile) by promising future glory to the city of Jerusalem. Despite opposition, God would bring his people back to the Holy City (40:6-8).

The theme of the remnant is prevalent throughout these chapters (46:3). The concept of the remnant was introduced early in Isaiah through the name of his sons. Isaiah named one son "Quick-to-the-Plunder-Swift-to-the-Spoil" as a symbol of God's judgment upon Judah. But his brother was named *Shear-Jashub*,

"A-Remnant-Will-Return," as a symbol of God's lasting faithfulness to his people. Isaiah 10:20-23 and 11:11-16 also express the remnant motif.

The remnant in exile would be a suffering remnant who were poor and mistreated and who longed for home. But how would they escape from Babylon, and where would they go when they escaped? Jerusalem was a city in ruin and the exiles doubted that God could redeem them. These chapters encourage the exiles to conquer their doubt and discouragement and to renew their faith in Yahweh. God pledged that he would send them aid in the form of deliverance (46:13). Since he once freed them from slavery in Egypt and brought them to a land of promise, he would again guarantee safe passage back to their homeland.

God was doing this because he loved his people, but he had another agenda as well. Using language reminiscent of, Hosea, Isaiah prophesied:

> For your Maker is your husband,
> the Lord of hosts is his name;
> and the Holy One of Israel is your Redeemer,
> the God of the whole earth he is called (Isaiah 54:5).

When the people returned, they were to praise God for their release so that all nations might know that the God of Israel is the true God (41:20). God was offering unconditional salvation to all of humanity. These chapters have been called "the Gospel of the Old Testament."

How would God bring about this deliverance? He was the Holy One of Israel. He had acted in their behalf in the past and would do so again. Since he governed all of creation, he could certainly free Judah. He would choose an instrument from the nations around Babylon who would initiate the release of his people. Isaiah 44:24-28 states:

> Thus says the Lord, your Redeemer,
> who formed you from the womb:

> *"I am the Lord, who made all things,*
> *who stretched out the heavens alone,*
> *who spread out the earth—Who was with me?—*
> *who frustrates the omens of liars,*
> *and makes fools of diviners;*
> *who turns wise men back,*
> *and makes their knowledge foolish;*
> *who confirms the word of his servant,*
> *and performs the counsel of his messengers;*
> *who says of Jerusalem, 'She shall be inhabited,'*
> *and of the cities of Judah, 'They shall be built,*
> *and I will raise up their ruins;'*
> *who says to the deep, 'Be dry,*
> *I will dry up your rivers;'*
> *who says of Cyrus, 'He is my shepherd,*
> *and he shall fulfill all my purpose;*
> *saying of Jerusalem, 'She shall be built,'*
> *and of the temple, 'Your foundation shall be laid.'"*

In 546 BC, Cyrus rose to power in Persia. Isaiah had prophesied years earlier that he would be the anointed shepherd who would return the exiles to Jerusalem (41:2-5; 42:25; 44:28; 45:1ff.; 46:11; 48:14-16). God worked through Cyrus to complete this vision for the people of Judah. The hope he instilled within Isaiah's heart two centuries earlier, now became reality.

Isaiah 56-66: Comfort for God's People

Isaiah 56-66 manifests a different tone from the preceding chapters. When the Jews reclaimed the Promised Land, they anticipated great and immediate blessings from God. Not all of these hopes were immediately realized. Many people in the post-exilic period suffered from a drought that had stricken the land, enemies who did not welcome their return and general conditions of poverty in the land. They found that upon their return that life was not rosy; instead, they had to work to rebuild life in Jerusalem.

Isaiah 61:1-3 announces:

> *The Spirit of the Sovereign*
> *Lord is on me,*
> *because the Lord has anointed me*
> *to preach good news to the poor.*
> *He has sent me to bind up the*
> *brokenhearted,*
> *to proclaim freedom for the*
> *captives*
> *and release from darkness for the*
> *prisoners,*
> *to proclaim the year of the Lord's*
> *favor*
> *and the day of vengeance of our*
> *God*
> *to comfort all who mourn,*
> *and provide for those who grieve*
> *in Zion*
> *to bestow on them a crown of*
> *beauty*
> *instead of ashes*
> *the oil of gladness*
> *instead of mourning,*
> *and a garment of praise*
> *instead of a spirit of despair.*
> *They will be called oaks of*
> *righteousness,*
> *a planting of the Lord*
> *for the display of his splendor.*

The Lord has ordered a year of jubilee in which all the debts will be canceled and all the land that had been wrested from the poor will be restored. God established the rights of the poor and took upon himself the burden of the oppressed (57:15). He cared for the simple and healed the wounds of the injured (65:21;

57:18). His desire was for justice and righteousness to thrive in the land.

C. God is Holy.

A central theme in Isaiah's work is the holiness of God. Isaiah is probably responsible for coining the phrase "Holy One of Israel" (1:4; 5:19, 24). The word "holy" can connote physical separation. It signifies the otherness of God. God is the Lord of creation and the Lord of history. He can manipulate the flow of history to suit his holy purpose. In Isaiah, this idea of otherness retains a flavor of God's glory and his love.

Isaiah experienced the holiness of God in his call (Isaiah 6:1-6). He knew of God's sovereignty from firsthand knowledge. Isaiah portrayed God as being in total and complete control of every nation of the world and every aspect of history. Whatever happened within the world was in his plan. Isaiah 14:24-27 reads:

> *The Lord of hosts has sworn;*
> *"As I have planned,*
> *so shall it be,*
> *and as I have purposed,*
> *so shall it stand,*
> *that I will break the Assyrian in*
> *my land,*
> *and upon my mountains trample*
> *him underfoot;*
> *and his yoke shall depart from them,*
> *and his burden from their shoulder."*
> *This is the purpose that is purposed*
> *concerning the whole earth;*
> *and this is the hand that is*
> *stretched out over all the nations.*
> *For the Lord of hosts has purposed,*
> *and who will annul it?*
> *His hand is stretched out,*
> *and who will turn it back?*

Since God controls the tides of human history, we should have confidence that he will work for our good. To attempt to manipulate events in your favor whether by turning to idols or by turning to foreign powers is an expression of unbelief. Isaiah's belief in the sovereignty of God compelled him to oppose alliances between Judah and Assyria or between Judah and Egypt. Isaiah viewed these moves as simple gestures of pride. By denying God and turning to foreign powers for aid, Judah would go the path of Samaria.

D. Yahweh is Creator and Redeemer.

The God who made Israel into a nation would redeem Israel out of bondage. This theme is expressed repeatedly in the book of Isaiah. Isaiah understood the creative activity of God as well as any other Old Testament prophet. Isaiah emphasized God's creative power by using the special verb of the Genesis account, *bara*. This verb implies an effortless creation. Yahweh, the God of Israel, laid the heavens in the sky and created humanity to populate the earth. Isaiah 40:12-21 extolled the greatness of God's creative power:

> *The Lord is the everlasting God,*
> *the Creator of the ends of the*
> *earth.*
> *He does not faint or grow weary,*
> *his understanding is unsearchable.*

Because of God's greatness, Israel could trust in God to continually bless it with his creative power. His power was made available to all who trusted in him.

> *He gives power to the faint,*
> *and to him who has no might he*
> *increases strength.*
> *Even youths shall faint and be*
> *weary,*

and young men shall fall
exhausted;
but they who wait for the Lord
shall renew their strength,
they shall mount up with wings
like eagles,
they shall run and not be weary,
they shall walk and not faint
(Isaiah 40:29-31).

Since God was the Creator and the Sovereign God, Israel could wait upon him in times of trouble, and he would give them strength to endure whatever they faced.

But God would not continually ask his people to endure without hope of salvation. God was Creator and Redeemer. He would redeem Israel out of her hopeless situations. The word redeemer (*go'el*) was taken from the realm of family law. When a family member was wronged, it was the duty of the *go'el* to bring justice to the situation. When a family member was forced to sell his property, the redeemer would buy it back and keep it within the family. In the case of murder, the *go'el haddam*, blood avenger, would seek out the murderer and avenge the death of his family member. For Israel, God stood as her champion who would vindicate her wrongs. Yahweh was to bring Israel out of exile and restore her to her former glory. He was to provide a new Exodus for her by taking her to a new Jerusalem. In this way God the Creator would also be God the Redeemer.

15. Messianic Expectations

The New Testament writers loved the book of Isaiah. They constantly used his work to substantiate the claim of Jesus' messiahship. O. T. Professor James A. Sanders has demonstrated the massive use of Isaiah in the New Testament by writing:

Isaiah is cited, alluded to, or otherwise appears in the New Testament more than any other Old Testament book. Five hundred and ninety references, explicit or otherwise, from sixty-three chapters of Isaiah are found in twenty-three New Testament books (239 from Isaiah 1-39; 240 from chapters 40-55; 111 from 56-66).[61]

The book of Isaiah, more than any other Old Testament book, helped the early church to understand the life, ministry, death and resurrection of Jesus. Isaiah is a preview of the Gospels. To study the book of Isaiah is to study the foundation of the New Testament. Isaiah truly was like John the Baptist—he prepared the way of the Lord.

16. Important Passages:

The Servant Songs.

Introduction.
Before we examine the Servant Songs, we will investigate the way the New Testament writers make use of the Old Testament in their writings. Clearly the Old Testament writers had a particular point they were making when they recorded their message. The New Testament writers do not always follow this point. Instead, they often make use of an Old Testament illusion to illustrate their own message. Often they use these images without being concerned if they are keeping true to the original point being made in the Old Testament text. The Old Testament writer was attempting to communicate God's will to his audience, and the New Testament writer was just as ambitious about communicating God to the people of his day. The New Testament writer may have been more concerned with using a particular word or phrase from an Old Testament text that meant something to his audience than with being true to the meaning of that phrase within the Old Testament text.

An example of this is the use of Isaiah 7:14 in Matthew 1:23. Isaiah is speaking to King Ahaz attempting to convince him not to enter into a military alliance with Rezin of Damascus and

Pekah of Israel against Tiglath-Pileser. Isaiah tells Ahaz that a son would be born of a young maiden and before he was able to choose his own food, Rezin and Pekah would be defeated. Assyria defeated Damascus in 732; therefore, Immanu-el must have been born in 734 BC.

Matthew takes what Isaiah said of this young boy named Immanu-el in the eighth century BC and applied it to person he knew of as Immanuel in his day and time. Because Matthew applied this text to Jesus it does not mean that Isaiah had Jesus in mind when he wrote it. Matthew could have applied this verse to Jesus as an allegory or a parallel to what Jesus would be in his day. This was a type, a boy born of a woman in the eighth century who served as a sign to Ahaz . The anti-type of this was Jesus who was born of a virgin for a sign to all of humanity.

How do the New Testament writers use
Old Testament scriptures?

(1.) Allegorically: Paul used Sarah and Hagar in this fashion in Galatians 4:24.

(2.) Typologically or Typically: The New Testament writers saw an image in the Old Testament as a type of what was to come in the New Testament age. For example, as Noah and his family were saved by the flood, this is a type of which baptism now saves us as an anti-type (1 Peter 3:21).

(3.) A Parallel or Analogy: The Old Testament event might parallel an event in the New Testament. Moses lifting up the serpent to save people in the wilderness parallels the lifting up of Jesus on the cross to save humanity.

(4.) An Accommodated Usage: The N. T. writer could have accommodated this reasoning to fit the line of reasoning used by the rabbis of their day. They could have borrowed from the midrash of Judaism or the pesher of the Qumran community.

(5.) A Secondary Meaning or Double Fulfillment: A legitimate Old Testament prophecy which was fulfilled in the Old Testament could have been used to speak of a second fulfillment

within the New Testament context. This is one way of understanding Isaiah 7:14. Isaiah mentions a child who must have been
born around 734 BC. Matthew picked up on this prophecy and
spoke of a second fulfillment of it in the birth of Jesus.

The New Testament writers often made use of the Old Testament to illustrate and substantiate points they were making.
How they used the Old Testament text depended upon the point
they were trying to make. The only way to properly determine
how the writer was using the text is to investigate each case in-
dividually.

Isaiah 42:1-4. The First Servant Song.
In this song Yahweh is making a pronouncement concerning the nature of his "Servant" who was to come. The text mentions both his "servant" Israel (vs. 1), the nations (vs. 2), and the
coastlands (vs. 4) as receiving the message. He is probably giving
a general pronouncement for all to hear.
Yahweh had Israel in mind as his servant in this passage. He
was looking forward to the time when Israel would influence the
nations around her and draw them to Yahweh.
Matthew applied the passage to Jesus in Matthew 12:17-21.
He could have been using this text in a number of ways including
parallel, typical or secondary fulfillment.
The servant, Israel, would serve as God's prophet to the nations. He would take the saving message of Yahweh to all of those
outside the covenant. God had endowed his servant with power
so that he might bring justice to the earth. This justice was the
true religion of Yahweh. It was based upon his teaching (Torah
or law).
The evangelism of the pagan nations around Israel would
not be accomplished by Israel's loud, boisterous proclamation.
Instead, Israel would be seen as a "bruised reed" or a "dimly
burning wick." Israel would accomplish her mission with compassion and empathy. She understood the condition of the nations because she had just suffered separation from God. She

had learned from experience the pain of separation. Now she could gently encourage the nations to embrace the true God of the nations.

Isaiah 49:1-6. The Second Servant Song.

Here the servant, Israel, related to the nations a conversation concerning Israel's mission. Although Israel was chosen from the womb to proclaim the word of Yahweh to the rest of the world, she had failed in her purpose. God must now raise her up anew so she could be a light to the nations.

The servant was to be a sword and a polished arrow used by Yahweh. She was an offensive weapon who would declare God's greatness. The nations were to see the power of God through her.

Israel was not just to proclaim the greatness of God to the nations. Much of Israel had forgotten God. The faithful were to remind Jacob (vs. 5) that God would gather them back to him.

Israel had always been chosen to reveal God to all of humanity (Gen. 22:18; 26:4; 28:14). God reminded Israel again that this was her purpose (42:1, 6; 44:5; 45:6, 14). Paul and Barnabas applied these verses to their ministry when they turned toward the Gentile mission after being rejected by the Jews in Antioch of Pisidia (Acts 13:47).

Isaiah 50:4-11. The Third Servant Song.

The question that rises from reading this text is who is the speaker? Anyone who has a working knowledge of the Gospels can easily place Jesus within the context because it is so descriptive of Christ. However, in this context it is better to see the speaker as the repentant exilic community that is personified as an individual. The remnant speaks to fellow exiles. Since he understands the hurt of abuse, he encourages a people being abused, urging them to trust in the Lord. The Servant was spit upon, and the hair of his beard was pulled out. In other words, he was held in utter contempt. Yet he endured the hardship because he trusted in God.

Isaiah 52:13-53:12. The Fourth Servant Song.
In this text a dramatic dialogue occurs which speaks to the Messianic nature of the Suffering Servant of the poem. The speakers are as follows:

(1.) 52:13-15. Yahweh speaks.

(2.) 53:1-6. The penitent Jewish exiles speak.

(3.) 53:7-9. Yahweh speaks.

(4.) 53:10-11a. The prophet speaks.

(5.) 53:11b-12. Yahweh speaks. The text begins and ends with God.

Who is the Suffering Servant? Although many suggestions have been made as to his identity, the only adequate answer is Jesus, the future Messiah. No one other than Jesus can meet all the points made within the text.

52:13-15. Yahweh informs his people that he will lift up his servant and glorify him. Although his condition now is undesirable, God will make him great. The contrast between his humiliation and his triumph will startle the nations. They will be taken aback because his physical form engenders feelings of weakness, but the servant will be made strong. He will accomplish the role that God desired of Israel, to inform the nations of his greatness.

This is reminiscent of the words of Jesus, "Though I be lifted up from the earth I will draw all men unto me." He displayed the power of God by being beaten and scarred. He took on the role of Israel becoming "the light" to the nations. He "startled nations and shut the mouths of kings." Jesus was unpredictable. He could not be pigeonholed into a single category. He was not what humanity expected as a Messiah because he was so much greater than what was expected.

53:1-3. Now the nations confess the difficulty of believing what they have seen. How could the powerful arm of the Lord be revealed in a servant who seemed so weak?

He had no form or comeliness that
we should look at him,
and no beauty that we should
desire him.

The servant did not attract people by his physical beauty or worldly charm. He was hideous and unbearable. The image is one of a leper from whom men hide their faces. Yet out of this weakness, God baffled the wisdom of the nations, for the Servant appeared before the people cloaked in a mystery, unrecognizable in his humiliation.

53:4-6. Why did the Servant suffer grief? Why was he despised and rejected? He suffered because he was Yahweh's chosen. Certainly he did nothing to deserve the humiliation he experienced.

He suffered for the sins of the nations. Notice how the writer shifts to the first person. It was not "men" who punished the servant, but "us." Eleven times in these three verses he uses personal pronouns. Jesus suffered because of us.

Surely he has borne our griefs
and carried our sorrows;
yet we esteemed him stricken,
smitten by God, and afflicted.
But he was wounded for our
transgressions,
he was bruised for our iniquities.

The one who was diseased becomes the source of wholeness and healing. He did not suffer because of his own shortcomings. He never failed (Heb. 4:15). He paid for our rebellion (I Peter 2:22).

He bore the sins of the one and the sins of the all. Isaiah states:

All we like sheep have gone astray;
we have turned every one to his
own way;
and the Lord has laid on him
the iniquity of us all.

53:7-9. How did Jesus bear up under the agony of his mission? Unlike most people who suffer, he did not cry out in bitterness and complaint. He endured his pain in silent contemplation of the glory to come.

Like a lamb that is led to the
slaughter,
and like a sheep that before its
shearer is dumb,
so he opened not his mouth.

He was led in his innocence through imprisonment, a mock trial and on to death. He never committed any violent act and a lie never passed his lips. Yet he died in complete loneliness separated from humanity and from divinity. The portrait of perfection was buried in a grave alongside the wicked.

53:10-12. Yahweh did not allow his Servant to continue in humiliation. The grave was unable to hold him. Yahweh glorified him before Israel, the nations and the universe.

The Servant could not complain about the road he traveled. He was not the recipient of ill-suited fate, but he was part of a divine scheme. His humiliation was an act of God. Yahweh purposed that he should suffer for the sins of humanity.

Yet it was the will of the Lord to
bruise him; ...
the will of the Lord shall prosper
in his hand.

Because the Servant gave himself for the transgressions of the world, he will be counted with the strong and the great.

God provided his own sacrifice for our sins. This was different from the Canaanite cultus where the individual had to placate a capricious god. God reached down in grace and corrected the situation for mankind. This great act is the single greatest event in all of human history. It serves as a constant reminder that "all we like sheep have gone astray." It also reminds us that the God of Israel is consistently there to plant our feet on the heights when we do stray.

Crucifixion to the World by the Cross of Christ
(Galatians 6:14)

When I survey the wondrous Cross
Where the young Prince of Glory died,
My richest gain I count but loss,
And pour contempt on all my pride.

Forbid it, Lord, that I should boast
Save in the death of Christ, my God;
All the vain things that charm me most,
I sacrifice them to his blood.

See from his head, his hands, his feet,
Sorrow and love flow mingled down;
Did e'er such love and sorrow meet?
Or thorns compose so rich a crown?

His dying crimson like a robe
Spreads o'er his body on the Tree,
Then am I dead to all the globe,
And all the globe is dead to me.

Were the whole realm of nature mine,
That were a present far too small;
Love so amazing, so divine,
Demands my soul, my life, my all.

—Isaac Watts
(1674-1748)

References

Baltzer, Klaus. *Deutero-Isaiah*. Hermeneia. 2001.

Beuken, W. *Isaiah. Part II, Vol. 2*. Historical Commentary on the Old Testament. 2000.

Blank, S. H. *Prophetic Faith in Isaiah*. 1958.

Childs, B. S. *Isaiah*. Old Testament Library. 2000.

_____. *Isaiah and the Assyrian Crisis*. 1967.

Goldinngay, John. *Isaiah*. New International Bible Commentary on the Old Testament. 2001.

Gordon, A. R. *The Faith of Isaiah*. 1919.

Herbert, A. S., *Isaiah 1-39*. 1973.

_____. *Isaiah 40-66*. 1975.

Kaiser, O. Translated by R. A. Wilson. *Isaiah 1-12*. 1972.

_____. *Isaiah 13-39*. 1974.

Kenneth, R. H. *The Composition of the Book of Isaiah in the Light of History and Archaeology*. 1910.

Margalioth, R. *The Indivisible Isaiah*. 1964.

Mauchline, J., *Isaiah 1-39*. 1962.

Motyer, Alec. *The Prophecy of Isaiah*. 1993.

North, C. R. *The Second Isaiah*. 1964.

Oswalt, J. *Isaiah. 2 Vols*. New International Commentary on the Old Testament. 1986, 1988.

Rowley, H. H. *The Servant of the Lord*. 1965.

Westermann, C. Translated by D.M.G. Stalker. *Isaiah 40-66*. Old Testament Library. 1969.

Whybray, R. N. *Isaiah 40-66*. New Century Bible Commentary. 1975.

Young, Edward. *The Book of Isaiah. 3 Vols*. 1965-1972.

7

Micah of Moresheth
The Prophet of the Poor

He has showed you, O man, what is good.
And what does the Lord require of you?
To act justly and to love mercy and
to walk humbly with your God
(Micah 6:8, NIV).

Micah does not rely on the human weapons of the revolutionary. He insists that Yahweh will reveal himself to his people, and when He does it will be to punish Judah's sin. For threat is the only possible issue, and Judah is rushing towards it at her highest speed. And his words found some echo in the conscience of his people, and a century later it was remembered that he had given warning and that men had staved off punishment by timely and thorough repentance.

—Theodore H. Robinson, OT scholar

1. Date

Micah prophesied in the days of Jotham (750-735), Ahaz (735-715) and Hezekiah (715-687), kings of Judah (1:1). Isaiah was active just prior to and during this time. Also, Micah was active just prior to, and somewhat after the fall of Samaria, capital of the Northern Kingdom (721 BC). Thus, he probably prophesied around 740-710 BC.

2. Location: Judah, the Southern Kingdom of Israel.

3. Purpose

Micah warned of God's coming judgment. He also announced God's sure mercy in the realization of Israel's salvation after judgment.

4. Theme: Destruction of both Samaria and Jerusalem was imminent because of their sinful state.

5. Meaning of Name

The name Micah is a shortened form of Micayaliu (cf. Judges 17:1, 4) and Micaiah (cf. I Kings 22:8) that means "Who is like Yahweh?" This is a rather common name in the Old Testament. At least nine different characters in the Old Testament books were named Micah. The name is very appropriate for the prophet Micah because he exalted Yahweh throughout his work.

6. Audience: Judah and Jerusalem.

7. Outline

> I. God's judgment on Samaria and Jerusalem (1:1-3:12)
> Title verse (1:1)
> A. The call to judgment (1:2-4)
> B. The general cause and consequence of the judgment (1:5-7)

C. Micah's concern for the judgment—a lament (1:8-16)
D. Specific causes of the judgment (2:1-3:12)

II. God's promise of deliverance for a remnant (4:1-8)
A. The effects of the coming exaltation of the Lord's house (4:1-8)
B. The sorrows of the present (4:9-5:1)
C. The advent of a deliverer (5:2-15)

III. God's controversy with his wayward people (6:1-7:20)
A. God makes a supreme appeal (6:1-8).
B. God condemns the evils of Jerusalem (6:9-16).
C. Micah laments the corruption of his people (7:1-6).
D. Micah affirms his faith in God (7:7-13).
E. Micah prays for his people (7:14-20).

8. Memory Work

Micah 4:1-3
In the last days
the mountain of the Lord's
temple will be established
as chief among the mountains;
it will be raised above the hills,
and peoples will stream to it.

Many nations will come and say,

"Come, let us go up to the
mountain of the Lord,
to the house of the God of Jacob.
He will teach us his ways,
so that we may walk in his
paths."

The law will go out from Zion,
the word of the Lord from
Jerusalem.
He will judge between many peoples
and will settle disputes for strong
nations far and wide.
They will beat their swords into
plowshares
and their spears into pruning
hooks.
Nation will not take up sword
against nation,
nor will they train for war
anymore (NIV).

Micah 5:2
But you, Bethlehem Ephrathah,
though you are small among the
clans of Judah,
out of you will come for me
one who will be ruler over
Israel,
whose origins are from of old,
from ancient times.

Micah 6:6-8
With what shall I come before the
Lord
and bow down before the exalted
God?
Shall I come before him with burnt
offerings,
with calves a year old?
Will the Lord be pleased with
thousands of rams,
with ten thousand rivers of oil?

Shall I offer my firstborn for my
transgression,
the fruit of my body for the sin of
my soul?
He has showed you, O man, what is
good.
And what does the Lord require
of you?
To act justly and to love mercy
and to walk humbly with your
God (NIV)

9. Special Notes

I. Micah and Isaiah: Micah spoke to the common man as a rustic evangelist and spoke of personal religion and social morality. Isaiah, on the other hand, often spoke to royalty as a courtier and statesman and spoke about political issues.

II. If Micah followed the tradition of prophetic symbolism as literally as Jeremiah or Ezekiel did, then he was a strange prophet indeed. Consider what he says in Micah 1:8:

Because of this I will weep and
wail;
I will go about barefoot and
naked.
I will howl like a jackal
And moan like an owl (NIV).

Also consider what he mentions in 1:16:

Shave your heads in mourning
for the children in whom you
delight;
make yourselves as bald as the
vulture,
for they will go from you into
exile (NIV).

If Micah is understood literally, then he walked through the streets of Jerusalem barefoot, naked and with a shaved head. This radical symbolism would draw attention to the prophetic message of the exile of Judah.

III. Speaking about the Hebrew text of Micah, R. K. Harrison notes, "Micah is in a good state of preservation, and is probably in the best condition of any of the eighth-century BC prophecies."[62]

10. Historical Context

Micah 1:1 informs us that Micah's ministry spanned the reigns of three kings of Judah. These three kings, Jotham (742-735 BC), Ahaz (735-715 BC) and Hezekiah (715-687 BC) allow for a fifty-five year period during which Micah could have prophesied. It is unlikely that Micah was active during the entire fifty-five years, and other events are mentioned that might narrow the time of his work.

Micah mentions Samaria (1:1, 6), idols, and Omri and Ahab (6:16) which lead us to believe that Micah began to prophesy before the fall of Samaria in 722 BC. Micah certainly was familiar with this period in Israel's history, and he chronicled the history with great similarity to Amos' work (compare Mic. 6:10-11 with Amos 8:5-6). The earliest identifiable reference in Micah's work is the march of Sennacherib from Lachish to Jerusalem in 701 BC (Micah 1:10-16). This places Micah's work toward the end of the eighth century BC. Jeremiah mentions that Micah predicted the fall of Jerusalem during the reign of King Hezekiah (715-687). Considering all these events, Micah's prophetic work could have taken place between the years 735 through 701, but he could have been active down through 687 BC.

Micah came upon the scene in a desperate time with a despairing message of doom. Under King Jotham, Judah enjoyed a time of economic prosperity and spiritual poverty. He was an ambitious king who forfeited the lives of the poor to build luxurious fortresses and palaces. King Ahaz, however, had to grapple with the iron hand of Assyrian domination. To ease the pressure from Assyria he levied heavy taxes on his people to pay tribute to Sennacherib. These taxes hit the poor the hardest as greedy landlords tightened the screws on the poor to pay their share of the taxes. King Hezekiah tried to reform Judah after taking Micah's message to heart. Yet Hezekiah could not turn the tide of corruption that was sweeping the land.

Micah was able to witness the collapse of the Northern Kingdom under the Assyrians. He would have been familiar with the deportation of the Israelites to Assyria as the men and women were stripped naked and chained together, often hooked through their buttocks to keep them in place. He knew of the Assyrians' ruthless treatment of their captives and he feared this treatment for the Southern Kingdom of Judah.

When Israel fell in 722 BC, Assyria began to assert itself on the Kingdom of Judah through military pressure and taxation. Whereas Assyria destroyed Samaria, it made a vassal nation out of Judah, extracting heavy tribute from both Ahaz and Hezekiah. This lighter treatment might have come because Judah did not side with Israel against Assyria during the Syro-Ephraimitic War, or it might have been the result of Judah's willingness to pay substantially for her freedom. Also, Judah was not as strategically significant as Samaria. Samaria was located on the main trade route between Asia and Africa. Jerusalem was a little hill state, which did not reach to the Mediterranean coast. Theodore H. Robinson notes the strategic difference:

> The great road, along which the merchandise of all the ages has moved, runs through the gap formed by Esdraelon in the Palestinian central range, and passes down the maritime plain, leaving Judah and Jerusalem away to the east behind the foothills. The world's traffic tended thus to pass her by. But at the same time, that position which was so advantageous to Samaria commercially proved in the end to be her ruin.[63]

Samaria was more valuable because she provided a buffer

between Assyria and Egypt. Judah, located more to one side, was not as strategically important and could stay out of trouble as long as she remained neutral to the affairs of the countries surrounding her.

After some time the Judeans grew tired of Assyria's taxes and sought a way to break free of her chains. Hezekiah, encouraged by Egypt, an enemy of Assyria, mounted an insurrection around the year 705. At this time Sennacherib (705-681 BC), the king of Assyria, was challenged by a coalition of tribes led by Merodach-baladan.[64] Merodach-baladan sought help from other countries to overthrow Sennacherib and the Assyrian power. Hezekiah seized this opportunity joining Tyre and Sidon in withholding tribute payments from Assyria. After Sennacherib had gained control of the eastern territories around Babylon, he turned his gaze west toward Judah.

After defeating the armies of Egypt and the Philistines, he defeated the city of Lachish and marched toward Jerusalem in 701 BC. II Kings 18-19 gives details about the Assyrian march on the capitol of Jerusalem. After gaining control of much of the countryside surrounding the capitol (Sennacherib boasted in his records of destroying forty-six Israelite cities in his march), Assyria laid siege to Jerusalem much as it had done to Samaria some 20 years earlier. This time Assyria was not as successful. King Hezekiah appealed to the prophet Isaiah for help to thwart the advance of their enemy. Isaiah assured Hezekiah that Jerusalem would not fall. II Kings 19:35-37 describes a sudden, massive destruction of the Assyrian forces surrounding Jerusalem. This could only be interpreted as God sparing Jerusalem from her enemies. Assyria lifted her siege of the city and returned home.

Micah noticed the same injustice in Judah that his fellow prophets, Amos and Hosea, had noticed in Samaria. Unlike Isaiah, Micah was a man of the country. He witnessed the burdens of the small farmer in the area of Moresheth-Gath. Micah 3:1-3 states:

> Hear, you heads of Jacob
> and rulers of the house of Israel!

Is it not for you to know justice?—
you who hate the good and love the evil,
who tear the skin from off my people,
and their flesh from off their bones;
who eat the flesh of my people,
and flay their skin from off them,
and break their bones in pieces,
and chop them up like meat in a kettle
like flesh in a cauldron.

According to Jeremiah 26:18-ff. Micah's message against Jerusalem so moved King Hezekiah that he entreated the Lord to save Jerusalem. Hezekiah's reforms spared Jerusalem for a time, but ultimately this city had to face the penalty of her sins.

11. The Person "Micah of Moresheth."

Moresheth-Gath, (Micah 1:14), was a small town located about 25 miles southwest of Jerusalem in the lower Shephelah (the foothill country). Micah's hometown was just 20 miles from Amos' birthplace, and this would help explain Amos' influence on Micah. Moresheth was situated on the main road between the Maritime Plain and Egypt, in the midst of very good farming land. This route served as a natural highway for the armies of Egypt to reach its enemies to the north and the east.

We know very little about the prophet Micah. Neither his occupation nor his father's name is mentioned in the book. Like Nahum the Elkoshite and Amos from Tekoa, Micah of Moresheth was known for his hometown. This implies that he no longer lived in his home village, and the people of Jerusalem identified him as being from a small town.

Some scholars suggest that Micah was an "elder of Judah" who administered justice in his home village;[65] others see military references in the book and suggest that he led the local militia in Moresheth.[66] Micah likely was a farmer who became incensed at the treatment of his compatriots to the point of taking up their cause by going to Jerusalem to prophesy. He connects with the sorrows and injustice experienced by the poor farmer, and he expressed indignation at their plight. He had little to say about the luxury and injustice of the big city though he did condemn it.

12. The Call

Micah never mentions a specific call, but he does allude to his call in Micah 3:7-8:

> *The seers shall be disgraced,*
> *   and the diviners put to shame;*
> *they shall all cover their lips,*
> *   for there is no answer from God.*
> *But as for me, I am filled with power,*
> *   with the Spirit of the Lord,*
> *and with justice and might,*
> *   to declare to Jacob his transgression*
> *and to Israel his sin.*

This prophetic consciousness led Micah through all of his ministry. He faced opposition like the other prophets, yet he stood firm (3:6, 11). The officials preferred pleasant words to Micah's harsh oracles (3:5, 11). Micah could hardly have had an easy life as a prophet of God. James D. Newsome, Jr., comments, "His total commitment to the prophetic calling compels him on at least one occasion to resort to bizarre behavior, if the words of 1:8 are to be taken literally. If he truly walked the streets of Jerusalem 'stripped and naked' as a sign of the coming judgment, he would have performed a feat similar to that of his great contemporary, Isaiah (Isaiah 20:2-4), two events which may, in fact, be related."[67]

13. Structure and Form

Within the book of Micah is the repetition of woe and weal that is seen in many other places in the Old Testament. This pattern of destruction and salvation, judgment and hope is also seen in Isaiah. The book can be divided into three sections:

(1.) Chapters 1-3: Judgment
(2.) Chapters 4-5: Hope
(3.) Chapters 6-7: Judgment and Hope

Puns (1:10-15): To show the advance of the Assyrian foe, Micah uses a long series of puns based upon the names of the towns near Jerusalem. James Moffatt and J. B. Phillips keep the meaning of these puns in their English translations. The following list offers an approximation:

Town	Meaning	Text
1. Gath	"tell town"	tell it not
2. Bethaphra	"dust town"	roll in the dust
3. Shaphir	"beautiful or fair town"	nakedness or shame
4. Zaanan	"march town"	march not forth
5. Bethezed	"neighbor or standing in place town"	no standing place
6. Maroth	"bitter town"	travail
7. Lachish	"horse town"	chariot
8. Moresheth-Gath	"betrothed of Gath town"	parting gifts
9. Aczib	"false spring town"	false brook
10. Mareshah	"heir town"	no heir
11. Adullam	"wild beast cave"	destruction

14. Theology
A. Because of Judah's sin, Zion will be destroyed.

Micah 3:12 is the keystone and climax of Micah's message of doom. Micah was one of the first prophets to prophesy against Jerusalem. The mistaken consensus of the people was that they were safe because of the Temple, and hence God's presence (3:11) was in their midst. Micah pronounced judgment against Jerusalem because of her sin. Since she had rebelled against God,

God would judge her. Her sins were many: idolatry (1:7; 5:12), murder (7:2), abuse of justice (2:1-2), stealing (6:11), lying (6:12) and turning to the occult (5:12). Judah's judgment was related to her crimes against God's people. Because God was just, he sought justice.

Micah pronounced severe judgment against God's sacred city:

> *Therefore, on your account*
> *Zion shall become a ploughed field,*
> *Jerusalem a heap of ruins,*
> *and the temple hill a rough heath*
> *(Micah 3:12, NEB).*

George L. Robinson, author of *The Twelve Minor Prophets*, sums up Micah's message in one sentence, "Those who live selfish and luxurious lives, even though they offer costly sacrifices, are vampires in the sight of God, sucking the life-blood of the poor."[68]

B. In the future God will glorify Zion (4:1-4).

In this section Jerusalem's spiritual destiny is contrasted with her present prospects. Hope did exist for Judah, but it was a hope that was oriented to the future. After she had paid the price for her sin, God would once again bless Jerusalem.

Micah 4-5 and 7:7-20 detail the future glory of Israel. God would bring a purified remnant out of the fire of judgment. He would give Israel a new king to be born in Bethlehem from the line of the great King David. This king would reign in majesty receiving the blessing of God and blessing the people. God would give the nation greater glory and prosperity than she had ever known. In fact:

> *Many nations shall come, and say:*
> *"Come, let us go up to the mountain of Yahweh,*
> *to the house of the God of Jacob;*

that he may teach us his ways
and we may walk in his paths."
For out of Zion shall go forth the law,
and the word of Yahweh from Jerusalem (Micah 4:2).

C. God's Demand (6:8).

Though the people multiplied sacrifices, they failed to understand the true nature of God's demands. In reality, Yahweh wanted his people to, "do justice, love kindness (i.e. steadfast love and covenant loyalty) and to walk humbly with their God." His main interest was in the heart, not the ritual. Compare 1 Samuel 15:22 that reads:

Has the Lord as great delight in
burnt offerings and sacrifices,
as in obeying the voice of the
Lord?
Behold, to obey is better than
sacrifice,
and to hearken than the fat of
rams.

15. Messianic Expectation

Bethlehem: Though Isaiah and Jeremiah prophesied concerning the Messiah (Isaiah 16:5; Jer.23:5; 33:15), Micah mentions the city in which he would be born. This was more than 700 years before the event. It is interesting to note that a poor prophet prophesied about a poor Messiah who would be born to a small, poor tribe, in a small, poor town.

16. Important Passages

God's Prerequisites

Micah 6:6-8

With what shall I come before the
    Lord
and bow down before the exalted
    God?
Shall I come before him with burnt
    offerings,
    with calves a year old?
Will the Lord be pleased with
    thousands of rams,
    with ten thousand rivers of oil?
Shall I offer my firstborn for my
    transgression,
the fruit of my body for the sin of
    my soul?
He has showed you, O man, what is
    good
And what does the Lord require
    of you?
To act justly and to love mercy
    and to walk humbly with your God.

This passage is the hallmark of the book of Micah and one of the great passages of the Old Testament. Bernhard W. Anderson calls it, "the epitome of the message of the eighth century prophets."[69] It is based on a covenant lawsuit where the Suzerain brought a complaint against his subject. The plaintiff sought damages for a breach of the covenant contract.

I. The Summons (6:1-2)

Micah begins chapter six by setting the scene as a court of law in which God is both the judge and the plaintiff. The mountains, the hills, and even the "everlasting foundations of the earth" will hear the testimony. God is sovereign over the world. No ordinary tribunal can hear his case, because he is not ordinary. The very nature of the case dictates an extraordinary court.

II. The Plaintiff's Charges (6:3-5)

God has a complaint against Israel. Israel has broken the covenant, and God is bringing her to court. When it is time for God to plead his case before creation, he turns to Israel and asks,

> *My people, what have I done to you?*
> *How have I burdened you?*
> *Answer me.*

You can see the tears in God's eyes as he lovingly looks over to Israel and asks, "Why?" God had provided for Israel's every need, cared for her in every situation, and loved her in spite of her constant rebellion. God wonders what he did wrong? Why is Israel acting this way? Many parents have sat up late at night with tears in their eyes asking the same question which God asks here, "How could I have done better?" "What did I do to drive him so far away?" "Why is she acting so rebelliously when all I've tried to do is love her?"

The difference between God and parents is that parents make mistakes. We often have to apologize to our children for mistakes we have made. God never made a mistake with Israel. He loved her with an unconditional love. He never had to say he was sorry for any of his actions. He acted only in Israel's best interest. His asks his question to make Israel reflect on her relationship with him. "Have I ever burdened you?" "Have I ever done anything that was not in your best interest?" If she were honest, Israel would have to answer, "No."

God calls to memory the times he saved Israel and treated her with kindness. He rehearses for her his mighty saving acts so she will remember his *hesed*—his saving grace. God recalls the time he saved Israel from the hand of the Egyptians who had shackled her in slavery. He reminds her of the great leaders he provided for her over the years to guide her along safe paths. He reminds Israel that he made other nations respect her by retelling the story of Balak. Balak, king of Moab, hired the seer Balaam to curse Israel because he feared this new nation. As Balaam goes to curse Israel, God directs him to bless Israel instead of cursing her. God cared for Israel to such an extent that the very curses which enemies hurled against Israel, God changed to blessing. He made her a mighty nation, and he gave her a fertile land blessing her journey from Shittim to Gilgal as she crossed the Jordan and into the land of promise.

Throughout the Old Testament Israel rehearsed the mighty acts of God and called to memory the events that made her great. The repetition of these acts were a part of her festivals and her worship. The Psalmists recorded these great deeds in psalms for Israel to sing so she would not forget that God had chosen her and not vice versa. Psalm 136 is a great responsorial psalm in which the cantor speaks of the mighty acts of God and the congregation responds, "His love endures forever."

We need to rehearse God's mighty deeds in our lives. We must never forget the ways that God has acted on our behalf to save us from the world and to bring us into his kingdom. We should sing of these acts and repeat them in our prayers and during times of meditation. Let's begin with the creation and remember all the great saving events of the Old Testament. Then we can move on to the birth of Jesus, his ministry and ultimately his death and resurrection. We can thank God for the ways he revealed himself through his apostles and his church. Then we can move through the centuries to the present day and the ways God has worked in our own lives. We need to mention events, people, times and places in which God has acted on our behalf. By doing this, we will be more thankful for God's mighty deeds.

III. The Defendant's Plea (6:6-7)

Israel responds to God's question by asking a few questions: "What do you expect of us?" "How do you want us to acknowledge you?" "We've kept up the rituals and our sacrifices haven't stopped. What exactly do you want?"

The very way she phrases her questions reveals her misunderstanding of God. She tried to please God with things—ritual acts that were meaningless. God was not interested in ritual. He desired a relationship with Israel.

The use of the words "come before" in verse 6 implies that two persons are meeting in relationship. The relationship is uniquely ordered however, because the next phrase speaks of Israel "bowing down" or "surrendering herself" before God in worship. Even though God could have forced Israel to bow before him, his nature would not allow it. He did not create robots that would simply whimper at the mention of his name. God created humanity with freedom and intellect so that humans could decide to follow him. He longs for a relationship with us, but he allows us the freedom to choose.

Israel lists the ways she thinks she can earn God's love. She begins with the simple and escalates to the sublime. Maybe a few sacrifices and burnt offerings would placate God. If not, then perhaps he might be interested in a thousand rams or 10,000 rivers of oil. These offerings recall the time Solomon at Gibeah offered 1,000 burnt offerings to God (I Kings 3:4). At the dedication of the temple at Jerusalem, Solomon offered 22,000 oxen and 120,000 sheep as sacrifices to Yahweh (I Kings 8:63). Would this suffice to earn God's care and attention? If not, then perhaps Israel should turn to the practices of the pagan religions around Palestine. Maybe an offering of a firstborn son would interest God? This hideous practice is not without precedent in the Old Testament. In Judges 11:34-40, Jephthah sacrificed his daughter to God to fulfill a vow he had made. Two kings of Judah, both King Ahaz and King Manasseh, offered up their sons to God (II Kings 16:3 and II Kings 21:6). Israel's understanding of God had become so perverted by foreign elements that she accepted into her worship what God had strictly prohibited in his law.

How could this have happened? Israel suffered the same delusion we suffer today. We feel that we have to perform great acts to merit God's love. We have been polluted by the world and its idea of love to the point that we have forced this view upon God. We cannot earn God's love. His love is freely given. Does the fact that he has given his love negate the need for prayer, evangelism or sacrifice? No, not in the least. We still do acts for God, not to merit anything, but because we are loved.

Think of your relationship with God as a marriage relationship (there is Biblical basis for this analogy in the book of Hosea). When you are married to someone, you do not perform the little acts of daily kindness to try to win their love. You have already chosen to love each other. You clean the dishes and take out the trash because you already are loved. You don't trade off tasks around the house and keep a list to accumulate points, saying, "You've done the dishes and made your side of the bed, but I've taken out the trash, mowed the yard, painted the gutters and made my side of the bed. My love is greater than yours and you owe me two favors before we are even." That is not love, and if this existed, it would signify an unhealthy relationship.

God has already chosen us. He loved us while we were in our mother's womb. We serve God because we are loved by God. We don't earn his love through service. His love is already present before we chose to serve him. We serve because we have been chosen. We serve because we are loved.

IV. The Indictment. (6:8)

Here we find, expressed in a single sentence, Amos's demand for justice, Hosea's appeal for the faithfulness that binds people in covenant with God and with one another, and Isaiah's plea for the quiet faith of the "humble walk" with God.[70]

—Bernhard W. Anderson, OT scholar

What does God require of us? Ralph L. Smith, author of an excellent commentary on the Minor Prophets, writes, "It is not so much what is in our hands but what is in our hearts that finds expression in our conduct that is important."[71] God desires our hearts. Hosea expressed God's desire in Hosea 6:6:

For I desire mercy, not sacrifice,
and acknowledgement of God
rather than burnt
offerings (NIV).

God wants us to acknowledge him. He wants us to let others know that he is the reason we are happy, together and complete. We should brag about God. It should become natural to talk to anyone about him because he has done so much for us.

How do we go about acknowledging God? Micah 6:8 mentions:

> To act justly and to love mercy
> and to walk humbly with your God (NIV).

Justice is the concept, mishpat, which calls for righteousness within the relationships of the covenant community. It is not enough to love God and go to a mountain to retreat from the world. Love of God must find expression in relationships that you attempt to make better every day. To love mercy (*hesed*) means that we will return to God the same unconditional love that he has lavished on us. By "walking humbly with your God" you recognize your dependence on God and your willingness to acknowledge him every day. Newsome sums this up by writing:

And so the movement within verse 8 is like this: God seeks from the worshiper justice (*mishpat*), or right relationships with one's brothers-and-sisters-in-community; kindness (*chesedh*), or a compassionate faithfulness toward others-in-community; and a humble walk with God, or the loving commitment of all that one is to the Almighty. Human relationships are listed first but are climaxed and embraced by one's relationship to God.[72]

With what shall I come before
    Yahweh
and bow down before the exalted
    God?
Shall I come before him with my
    prayer list,
        with quiet times for the past year.
Will Yahweh be pleased with

thousands of invitations to Bible talk,
with ten thousand invitations to a
"Bring Your Neighbor Day."

Shall I offer my time with my children
for my transgression,
time with my wife for the sin of my soul?

He has showed you, O man, what is
good.
And what does the Lord require of you?
To treat each other with fairness and equity.
To shower yourself with God's grace,
as you live each day acknowledging
the majesty of
Yahweh your God.
—G. Steve Kinnard, Nov. 1991

References

Anderson, F. and D. Freedman. *Micah*. Anchor Bible. 2000.

Copass, B. A. and E. L. Carson. *A Study of the Prophet Micah*. 1950.

Hillers, D. *Micah*. Hermeneia. 1983.

Marsh, J. *Amos and Micah*. Tyndale Bible Commentary. 1959.

Mays, J. L. *Micah*. Old Testament Library. 1976.

McKane, W. *Micah*. International Critical Commentary. 1998.

McKeating, H. *Amos, Hosea, Micah*. 1971.

Smith, Ralph L. *Micah-Malachi*. 1984.

Snaith, N. *Amos, Hosea, Micah*. 1956.

Wolf, H. *Micah*. Continental. 1990.

_____. *Micah the Prophet*. 1981.

End Notes

1. G. Steve Kinnard, *Prophets: The Voices of Yahweh* (Billerica, Mass.: Discipleship Publications International, 2001), p. 11.

2. Peter C. Craigie, *Twelve Prophets, Vol. 1,* The Daily Study Bible Series (Philadelphia: The Westminster Press, 1994), p. 86.

3. Douglas Stuart, *Hosea-Jonah,* Word Biblical Commentary (Waco, Texas: Word Books, Publisher, 1987), p. 226.

4. Craigie, p. 86.

5. Stuart, p. 227.

6. Stuart, p. 408.

7. Ibid., p. 404.

8. Craigie, p. 195.

9. Stuart, p. 403.

10. From Stuart, pp. 405-406.

11. Craigie, p. 195.

12. James D. Newsome, Jr., *The Hebrew Prophets* (Atlanta: John Knox Press, 1984), p. 16.

13. John Bright, *A History of Israel, 3rd ed.* (Philadelphia: The Westminster Press, 1972), p. 252.

14. Alberto Soggin, "The Davidic-Solomonic Kingdom," *Israelite and Judean History,* Eds. John H. Hayes and Maxwell Miller (Philadelphia: The Westminster Press, 1970), p. 417.

15. Ibid., p. 433.

16. George W. Anderson, *A Critical Introduction of the Old Testament* (London, Gerald Duckworth & Co., Ltd., 1959), p. 150.

17. Norman H. Snaith, *The Book of Amos, Vol. I* (London: The Epworth Press, 1945), p. 15.

18. Gleason L. Archer, *A Survey of Old Testament Introduction* (Chicago: Moody Press, 1964), p. 316.

19. W. O. E. Oesterly and Theodore H. Robinson, *An Introduction to the Books of the Old Testament* (New York: The Macmillian Co., 1934), p. 366.

20. William Rainey Harper, *Amos and Hosea,* The International Critical Commentary (Edinburgh: T&T Clark, 1905), p. 3

21. John D.W. Watts, "*Amos, The Man,*" Review and Expositor 63 (Fall 1966): 389.

22. Abraham J. Heschel, *The Prophets, Volume I* (New York: Harper and Row, Publ., 1962), p. 38.

23. George W. Anderson, p. 150.

24. Brevard S. Childs, *Introduction to the Old Testament as Scripture* (Philadelphia, Fortress Press, 1979), p. 405.

25. George L. Robinson, *The Twelve Minor Prophets* (New York: George H. Coran Company, 1926), p. 52.

26. Heschel, vol. I, p. 37.

27. Gerhard von Rad, *Old Testament Theology, vol. II*, translated by D.M.G. Stalker (New York: Harper & Row, Publ., 1965), p. 135.

28. Theodore H. Robinson, p. 149.

29. Stuart, p. 431.

30. John D. W. Watts, *The Books of Joel, Obadiah, Jonah, Nahum, Habakkuk, and Zephaniah*, The Cambridge Bible Commentary (Cambridge: University Printing House), p. 72.

31. Peter C. Craigie, *Twelve Prophets, vol. 1*, The Daily Study Bible Series (Philadelphia: The Westminster Press, 1984), p. 213.

32. John D. W. Watts, p. 74.

33. Theodore H. Robinson, p. 150.

34. I wonder if seafood ever tasted the same for Jonah again.

35. Douglas Stuart, p. 435.

36. Theodore H. Robinson, p. 77.

37. E. W. Heaton, *The Old Testament Prophets* (Atlanta: John Knox Press, 1977), p. 93.

38. John F. A. Sawyer, *Prophecy and the Prophets of the Old Testament*, (Oxford: Oxford University Press, 1987), pp. 106-107.

39. T. H. Robinson, pp. 72-73.

40. T. H. Robinson, p. 79.

41. Words in parentheses are the author's.

42. Klaus Koch, *The Prophets: Volume One—The Assyrian Period* (Philadelphia: Fortress Press, 1978), p. 79.

43. James D. Newsome, Jr., *The Hebrew Prophets* (Atlanta: The John Knox Press, 1984) pp. 34 35. Newsome states his indebtedness for this list to Hans Walter Wolff, *Hosea*, Hermeneia, translated by Gary Stansell (Philadelphia: Fortress Press, 1974), p. xxiv.

44. B. W. Anderson, *Understanding the Old Testament, 4th Ed.* (Englewood Cliffs, New Jersey: Prentice Hall, 1986), p. 302.

45. George L. Robinson, *The Twelve Minor Prophets* (New York: George H. Doran Company, 1926), p. 16.

46. Theodore H. Robinson, p. 77.

47. George L. Robinson, p. 17.

48. Stuart, p. 53.

49. Newsome, p. 40.

50. Theodore H. Robinson, pp. 98-99.

51. Gleason L. Archer Jr., *A Survey of the Old Testament* (Chicago: Moody Press, 1974), p. 332.

52. Ibid, p. 336.

53. Roland Kenneth Harrison, *Introduction to the Old Testament* (Grand Rapids, Michigan: William B. Eerdmans Publ. Co., 1969), p. 777.

54. Archer, pp. 348-351.

227

55. Harrison, p. 790.
56. Ibid.
57. Archer, p. 351.
58. Klaus Koch, *The Prophets, Vol. One: The Assyrian Period,* Trans. by Margaret Kohl (Philadelphia: Fortress Press, 1983), p. 107.
59. Theodore H. Robinson, p. 95.
60. Archer, p. 329.
61. James A. Sanders, "Isaiah in Luke," *Interpreting the Prophets,* edited by James Luther Mays and Paul J. Achtemeier (Philadelphia: Fortress Press, 1987), p. 75.
62. Harrison, p. 215.
63. Theodore H. Robinson, p. 89.
64. Ralph L. Smith, *Micah-Malachi* (Waco, Texas: Word Books, Publisher, 1984), p. 5.
65. Newsome, p. 48.
66. Koch, p. 95.
67. Newsome, p. 47.
68. George L. Robinson, p. 97.
69. Bernhard W. Anderson, *Understanding the Old Testament,* 4th Ed. (Englewood Cliffs, New Jersey: Prentice-Hall, 1986), p. 247.
70. Anderson, p. 247.
71. Ralph Smith, p. 10.
72. Newsome, p. 57.

Bibliography

Achtemeier, Elizabeth. *Nahum-Malachi*. Interpretation: A Bible Commentary for Teaching and Preaching. Atlanta: John Knox Press, 1986.

Ahoroni, Y. *The Archaeology of the Land of Israel*. London, [no publisher], 1982.

———. *The Land of The Bible*. Second Edition. Philadelphia: Fortress, 1979.

Albright, W. F. *The Archaeology of Palestine and the Bible*, reprinted by the American Schools of Oriental Research, 1974 . Original Edition. University of Virginia, 1931.

The American Heritage Dictionary. 3rd Ed. Edited by Anne H. Soukhanov. Boston: Houghton Mifflin Company, 1992.

Anderson, Bernhard W. *Understanding the Old Testament*. 4th Ed. Englewood Cliffs, New Jersey: Prentice-Hall, 1986.

Anderson, George W. *A Critical Introduction of the Old Testament*. London: Gerald Duckworth and Co., Ltd., 1959.

Archer, Gleason L., Jr. *A Survey of the Old Testament Introduction*. Chicago: Moody Press, 1974.

Ash, Anthony L. *Jeremiah and Lamentations*. Abilene, Texas: Abilene Christian University, 1987.

Barth, Christoph. *God with Us*. Edited by Geoffrey W. Bromiley. Grand Rapids, Michigan: William B. Eerdmans Publishing Company, 1991.

Ben-Arieh, Y. *The Rediscovery of the Holy Land in the Nineteenth Century*. Jerusalem: Magnes Press, 1989.

Bright, John. *A History of Israel*. 3rd Ed. Philadelphia: The Westminster Press, 1981.

Brueggemann, Walter. *The Prophetic Imagination*. Philadelphia: The Fortress Press, 1978.

———. *To Pluck Up, To Tear Down—Jeremiah 1-25*. Grand Rapids, Michigan: Wm. B. Eerdmans Publ. Co., 1988.

Buechner, Frederick. *Peculiar Treasures: A Biblical Who's Who*. San Francisco: Harper & Row, Publ., 1979.

Childs, Brevard S. *Introduction to the Old Testament as Scripture*. Philadelphia: Fortress Press, 1979.

Chisholm, Robert. *Handbook on the Prophets*. Grand Rapids, Mich.: Baker Book House, 2002.

Craigie, Peter C. *Ezekiel*. The Daily Study Bible Series. Philadelphia: The Westminster Press, 1983.

———. *Twelve Prophets*. Vols. I and II. The Daily Study Bible Series. Philadelphia: The Westminster Press, 1984.

Culver, Robert D. "nabi." In *Theological Wordbook of the Old Testament*. Edited by R. Laird Harris. Chicago: Moody Press, 1980: 1275.

Cunliffe-Jones, H. *A Word for Our Time?* London: The Athlone Press, 1973.

Davidson, Robert. *Jeremiah*. Vols. I and II. The Daily Study Bible Series. Philadelphia: The Westminster Press, 1983.

Dillard, Raymond, and Tremper Longman. *Introduction to the Old Testament*. Grand Rapids, Mich: Zondervan, 1994.

Driver, S. R. *The Minor Prophets*. Edinburgh: Cambridge University Press, 1896.

Drumbrell, William. *The Faith of Israel*. Grand Rapids, Mich.: Baker Book House, 2002.

Eichrodt, Walther. *Ezekiel*. The Old Testament Library. Translated by Cosslett Quin. Philadelphia: The Westminster Press, 1970.

_____. *Theology of the Old Testament*. Vols. I and II. Translated by J. A. Baker. Philadelphia: The Westminster Press, 1961.

Finegan, Jack. *Myth and Mystery*. Grand Rapids, Michigan: Baker Book House, 1989.

Harper, William Rainey. *Amos and Hosea*. The International Critical Commentary. Edinburgh: T&T Clark, 1905.

Harrison, Roland Kenneth. *Introduction to the Old Testament*. Grand Rapids, Michigan: William B. Eerdmans Publishing Co., 1969.

Hayes, John H. and J. Maxwell Miller, Editors. *Israelite and Judaean History*. Philadelphia: The Westminster Press, 1977.

Heaton, E. W. *The Book of Daniel*. Torch Commentaries. London: SCM Press, 1956.

_____. *The Old Testament Prophets*. Atlanta: John Knox Press, 1977.

Heschel, Abraham J. *The Prophets*. Vols. I and II. New York: Harper & Row, Publ., 1962.

Holladay, Jr., John S. "Assyrian Statecraft and the Prophets of Israel." In *Prophecy in Israel*. Edited by David L. Peterson. Philadelphia: Fortress Press, 1987: 122-143.

The Jerusalem Bible. New York: Doubleday & Co., Inc., 1966.

Kinnard, G. Steve. *The Beginning of Wisdom*. New York: The New York City Church of Christ, 1988.

_____. *The Call of the Wise: An Introduction and Topical Index to the Book of Proverbs*. Woburn, Mass.: Discipleship Publications International, 1997.

_____. *The Crowning of the King: A Practical Exposition of the Gospel of Matthew*. Newton, Mass.: Illuminations Publishers International, 2004.

_____. *The Final Act: A Biblical Look at End-Time Prophecy*. Woburn, Mass: Discipleship Publications International, 2000.

_____. *Getting the Most From the Bible*. Woburn, Mass: Discipleship Publications International, 2000.

_____. *The Gospel of Mark: An Introduction to Discipleship*. Woburn, Mass: Discipleship Publications International, 1995.

_____. *Holy Land Tour: The Gihon Spring*. (Video). New City, New York: G. Steve Kinnard, 2000.

_____. *Jerusalem: City of Promise*. (Video). New City, New York: G. Steve Kinnard, 1999.

_____. *New Wineskins: Formation of a Ministry of Multimedia Education Integrating the Bible, Geography and Archaeology*. New City: New York: G. Steve Kinnard, 1999.

_____. *Prophets: The Voices of Yahweh*. Billerica, Mass: Discipleship Publications International, 2001.

_____. *The Way of the Heart*. Spring, Texas: Illuminations Publishers International, 2006.

_____. *Walking the Way of the Heart*. Spring, Texas: Illuminations Publishers International, 2006.

_____. Editor. *Undivided Devotion*. Billerica: Mass: Discipleship Publications International, 2002.

Kinnard, G. Steve and Sifu Karl Romain. *The Cross and the Warrior*. Spring, Texas: Theatron Press, 2006.

Kirkpatrick, A. F. *The Doctrine of the Prophets*. London: MacMillian and Co., Limited, 1897.

Koch, Klaus. *The Prophets: Volume One—The Assyrian Period*. Translated by Margaret Kohl. Philadelphia: Fortress Press, 1983.

LaSor, William, David Hubbard, and Frederic Bush. *Old Testament Survey*. Second Edition. Grand Rapids, Mich.: Eerdmans, 1996.

Lindblom, J. *Prophecy In Ancient Israel*. Philadelphia: Fortress Press, 1962.

_____. "The Lives of the Prophets." *Journal of Old Testament Literature*, Monograph 1, 1946.

Luthi, Walter. *The Church to Come*. English Edition. London: Hodder & Stoughton, 1939.

Manson, T. W., Editor. *A Companion to the Bible*. Edinburgh: T & T Clark, 1939.

Mays, Luther James and Paul J. Achtemeier, Editors. *Interpreting the Prophets*. Philadelphia: Fortress Press, 1987.

Moorey, P. R. S. *A Century of Biblical Archaeology*. Louisville, Kentucky: Westminster/John Knox Press, 1991.

Mowvley, Harry. *Reading the Old Testament Prophets Today*. Atlanta: John Knox Press, 1979.

Napier, B. D. *Prophets In Perspective*. New York: Abingdon Press, 1962.

The New English Bible with the Apocrypha. New York: Cambridge University Press, 1972.

The New International Bible. Nashville: Holman Bible Publishers, 1986.

Newsome, James D., Jr. *By The Waters of Babylon*. Atlanta: John Knox Press, 1979.

_____. *The Hebrew Prophets*. Atlanta: John Knox Press, 1984.

Oesterly, W. O. E. and Theodore H. Robinson. *An Introduction to the Books of the Old Testament*. New York: The Macmillian Co., 1934.

Petersen, David. *The Prophetic Literature*. Philadelphia: Westminster John Knox, 2002.

Pieffer, Charles F. *Old Testament History*. Grand Rapids, Michigan: Baker Book House, 1973.

Pitt-Watson, Ian. *A Kind of Folly*. [no publisher, no place] 1976

The Revised Standard Version. [no place]: Division of Christian Education of the National Council of the Churches of Christ in the United States of America, 1971.

Robinson, George L. *The Twelve Minor Prophets*. New York: George H. Doran Company, 1926.

Robinson, H. Wheeler. *The History of Israel*. London: Gerald Duckworth & Co. Ltd., 1938.

_____. *Religious Ideas of the Old Testament*. Studies in Theology. London: Gerald Duckworth & Co. Ltd., 1959.

Robinson, Theodore H. *Prophecy and the Prophets in Ancient Israel*. New York: Charles Scribner's Sons, 1923.

Rosenberg, David. *A Poet's Bible*. New York: Hyperion, 1991.

Russell, D. S. *Daniel.* The Daily Study Bible Series. Philadelphia: The Westminster Press, 1981.

_____. *Daniel—An Active Volcano.* Louisville, Kentucky: Westminister/John Knox Press, 1989.

Sanders, James A. "Isaiah in Luke." In *Interpreting the Prophets.* Edited by James Luther Mays and Paul J. Achtemeier. Philadelphia: Fortress Press, 1987.

Sawyer, John F. A. *Isaiah.* Vols. I and II. The Daily Study Bible Series. Philadelphia: The Westminster Press, 1984.

Sawyer, John F. A. *Prophecy and the Prophets of the Old Testament.* Oxford: Oxford University Press, 1987.

Scott, R. B. Y. *The Relevance of the Prophets.* Rev. Ed. New York: Macmillan Publ. Co., 1973.

Sklba, Richard J. *Pre-Exilic Prophecy. Message of Biblical Spirituality.* Collegeville, Minn.: The Liturgical Press, 1990.

Smith, J. M. Ponis, *The Prophets and Their Times.* Chicago: The University of Chicago Press, 1925.

Smith, Ralph L. *Micah—Malachi.* Waco, Texas: Word Book Publishers, 1994.

Snaith, Norman H. *The Book of Amos.* Vol. 1. London: The Epworth Press, 1945.

Soggin, Alberto. "The Davidic-Solomonic Kingdom." In *Israelite and Judean History.* Edited by John H. Hayes and Maxwell Miller. Philadelphia: The Westminster Press, 1970.

Stuart, Douglas. *Hosea—Jonah.* Word Biblical Commentary. Waco, Tex.: Word Books, Publisher, 1987.

Tanakh—The Holy Scriptures. Philadelphia: The Jewish Publication Society, 1985.

Terrien, Samuel. *The Elusive Presence.* Religious Perspectives. New York: Harper & Row Publishers, 1978.

Watts, John D. W. "Amos, The Man." *Review and Expositor:* 102.

_____. *The Books of Joel, Obadiah, Jonah, Nahum, Habakkuk, and Zephaniah.* The Cambridge Bible Commentary. Cambridge: University Printing House, 1974.

Wilson, Ian. *The Bible Is History.* Washington: Regnery Publishing, Inc., 1999.

Wolff, Hans Walter. *Hosea.* Hermeneia. Translated by Gary Stansell. Philadelphia: Fortress Press, 1974.

Wright, G. Ernest. *God Who Acts.* Chicago: Alec R. Allenson, Inc., 1952.

Yancy, Philip. *The Bible Jesus Read.* Grand Rapids, Mich.: Zondervan Publishing House, 1999.

VanGemeren, Willem. *Interpreting the Prophetic Word.* Grand Rapids, Mich.: Zondervan 1990.

Von Rad, Gerhard. *Old Testament Theology.* Vols. I and II. Translated by D. M. G. Stalker. New York: Harper and Row, Publ., 1965.

Zimmerli, Walter. *The Law and the Prophets.* Translated by R. E. Clements. Oxford: Blackwell, 1965.

Illumination Publishers International

Toney Mulhollan has been in Christian publishing for over 30 years. He has served as the Production Manager for Crossroads Publications, Discipleship Magazine/ UpsideDown Magazine, Discipleship Publications International (DPI) and on the production teams of Campus Journal, Biblical Discipleship Quarterly, Bible Illustrator and others. He has served as production manager for several printing companies. Toney serves as the Editor of Illumination Publishers International. Toney is happily married to the love of his life, Denise Leonard Mulhollan, M.D. They make their home in Houston, Texas along with their daughter, Audra Joan.

For the best in Christian writing and audio instruction, go to the Illumination Publishers International website. We're commited to producing in-depth teaching that will inform, inspire and encourage Christians to a deeper and more committed walk with God. You can reach Toney Mulhollan by email at toneyipibooks@mac.com or at his office number, (832) 559-3658.

www.ipibooks.com

Breinigsville, PA USA
26 November 2009
228202BV00003B/1/P